Read *my* Lips

How to Achieve Your Life, Health & Wealth Goals

Ladies Initiating
Prosperity & Success

www.ReadMyLips.com

lips
Ladies Initiating
Prosperity&Success

Mail: PO Box 1171 Mooloolaba, Queensland, 4557 Australia
Email: info@readmylips.com
Web: www.ReadMyLips.com

First Published 14 February 2006
Revised August 2008

Copyright © LIPS Group PTY LTD 2008 ABN: 90 132 412 894

The moral right of the authors have been asserted. The stories, suggestions and opinions of the authors are their personal views only. We do not suggest in any way that every strategy will work for every person. They are the authors' thoughts only. Due diligence is always recommended.

All rights reserved. Without limiting the rights under copyright reserved above, no part of this publication may be reproduced, stored in or introduced into a retrieval system, or transmitted, in any form or by any means (electronic, mechanical, photocopying, recording, or otherwise), without the prior written permission of the authors and the publisher of this book.

Cover Design: Jenny Smallwood rusnjen@bigpond.net.au
Editing: Kristine Olsson
Typesetting & Layout: Blue Crystal Creative, www.BlueCrystalCreative.com
Printed and Bound: McPhersons Printing Group, www.mcphersonsprinting.com.au
Australian Distributor: Gary Allen Pty Ltd, customerservice@garyallen.com.au

ISBN 978-0-9751796-1-1

Contents

Every Success	2
About LIPS	3
CHAPTERS	
Life	**10**
Achieving Success – Consciously Creating the Life you want	11
Becoming your Authentic Self	24
Who Am I? Who Are You? Personality Profiling	31
Life Balance -Time Management	55
Declutter (Lighten) Your Life	62
Planning Your Road Map To Success	67
Health	**73**
The Real Truth About Food	74
Healthy Body – Healthy Mind	80
Mood, Foods and the Mind	85
The Truth on Beauty	93
Superwoman Survival	110
Get your Body Moving	120
Wealth	**128**
The Truth On Wealth	129
3 Steps to Financial Freedom	140
Great Investment Strategies	153
Creating an Income from Home	165
LIPS Manifesto	180
Beautiful LIPS Women	185
Acknowledgements	**187**
Rachael Bermingham	188
Cyndi O'Meara	189
Kim Morrison & Fleur Whelligan	190
Jodie McIver	191
Allison Mooney	192
Author Profiles	**193**
Rachael Bermingham	194
Cyndi O'Meara	196
Kim Morrison & Fleur Whelligan	198
Jodie McIver	200
Allison Mooney	202
Bibliography	204

Every Success

Every single success you have ever achieved required action and implementation. To change your world you first need to change yourself and this is not for the fainthearted. But know this: if you weren't up to the task then this book would never have found you. So be brave, be strong, love and value yourself.

Go out there and be who you really are and live the life you've always desired.

It is our hope that these strategies that have served *us* well, will also take *you* where you wish to go. Congratulations on taking some time out for *you* to inspire yourself to create a better life for you and your family.

Every Success!

Rachael, Cyndi, Kim, Fleur, Jodie and Allison

A foreword by Cyndi O'Meara...

What this book is about, and how it can help you find, achieve and live your dreams.

It's amazing what you can accomplish when you put your heart and mind to something that you really want to do. This book is written by a group of sensational women who have done just that and made a difference, not only in their own lives but in the lives of many others.

I think it is appropriate to start from the beginning. Rachael Bermingham is someone with talent, and her most impressive talents are passion, persistence and getting the job done. And, she does this in a very systemised and organised way. I have never seen anyone accomplish what she can in any given time and still keep a smile. She is one of those positive people who never says 'die' or 'stop'.

I met Rachael at a seminar where we were both speaking and we struck up a friendship. Not long after that meeting Rachael announced she was pregnant with her first child. My first thought was, 'that will slow her down', but there was never a thought more wrong. Soon (days) after the birth of her son she asked if I was interested in doing a seminar with her. She had found a few ladies who would be perfect for a seminar series for women.

Her goal was to teach women who were still at home with children that they could not only be successful mothers and wives, but also that they could build a business (or income) from their own passion, preferably from home. For me this was an exciting project. I was someone who spent most of my days alone in my home office without too much interaction, except when I was speaking or doing a book launch. To be involved with a group of women with the same philosophy and principles meant that I could bounce ideas off, and shine with, women who wanted to run. I knew that my life was meant for more than I was doing. I knew, like Rachael, that my life had to have meaning and that I wanted to make a difference in the world.

Rachael called the first meeting and we all met at my house; four women were present. That meeting was the beginning of a revolution; a revolution to help women find their passion and energy in order to create the life they wanted *rather* than the life they were living. A **(LIPS)** revolution, so women could start taking back their lives, start *taking control* of their life rather than having life *happen* to them! We had many talents including a financial whiz, decluttering queen, time management guru, health and beauty experts... we had all bases covered!

Rachael was the brilliance behind building businesses using clever marketing and business ideas (all on zero dollar budget), as well as helping people find their passion, achieve their goals and live extraordinary lives. My specialty is to inspire people to get healthy and live with abundant energy so they can do what they want to do – you see most people are so tired, the mere *thought* of making their life extraordinary puts them to sleep!

What happened at that meeting was nothing less than extraordinary. We each naturally assumed and took up our roles of what we were best at within the meeting. From that meeting came our vision and mission statements:

A foreword by Cyndi O'Meara...

> **Vision: Life and Wealth Success Strategies for Real Women**
>
> **Mission: To awaken women's natural skills and talents to achieve an income whilst fulfilling all facets of their life.**

The meeting ended with excitement and a sense of achievement. The next day emails between the four of us ran riot. Rachael, after looking at all our key words, came up with the most wonderful acronym. **LIPS** – Ladies into Prosperity and Success – which transformed into **Ladies Initiating Prosperity and Success.** And that was exactly what we all became, and who we *still* are and what we happily *still* do!

Weekly meetings were the result of that one day, marketing was hot, systems were put into place, the date for our first seminar was set and things moved along amazingly swiftly. One idea put into action can be a very powerful project.

Six weeks later on the beautiful Sunshine Coast in Queensland (Australia), we had our first LIPS seminar. It was a great success with rave reviews. By the end of the day most of the women in the room who had come with no idea about what they wanted to do in their lives, had a really good idea of what they wanted and were excited to get started in achieving it straight away.

At the end of the seminar we asked people to make commitments to themselves and we partnered them up so that they could help each other with their commitment. A very successful strategy! What was amazing was that many of the women who partnered together realised how they could each assist each other in the tasks they needed to do in order to create the business and life they wanted.

By the way, we not only created this impressive and successful business together in just five months, we did it all without spending a cent! That's right; not one cent came from *any* of our pockets, and we hosted five seminars, the contents of which have now evolved into

A foreword by Cyndi O'Meara...

this book you are now reading, (and revised and updated in a second edition), recorded and produced two audios, and the profits also paid for this book you are reading as well, all with a 'time only' investment. Pretty great for around 4-10 hours per week on average!

In any business, new concepts evolve so we decided to gather ladies who would be LIPS presenters and write this book to inspire women just like you, and show steps that can help you reach your potential and your goals. We knew that without sacrificing our own personal big pictures and goals, (not to mention our relationships and health) it was physically impossible to take our seminar to all the destinations around the world where women need this information, so to get our message out there, **Read My Lips** was written.

At the conference where Rachael and I met, we were introduced to two dynamic ladies, Kim Morrison and Fleur Whelligan, who were doing wonderful things for women in New Zealand and had written two books, *Like Chocolate For Women* and *Like An Apple A Day*. Their passion in life is teaching women how to nurture, love and look after themselves naturally and holistically. And so we asked them to be LIPS presenters and to contribute to the creation of this book.

Kim and Fleur then introduced us to another remarkable lady who helps women with relationships on every level. Allie Mooney's speciality is teaching people to understand different personality types and the way to put that knowledge into practice by meeting the needs of different personalities as well as communicating with them on their level. Allie became the fifth contributor to Read My Lips and is a perfect fit with the LIPS team and our philosophy.

The sixth contributor and member to the LIPS team is Jodie McIver. We met Jodie via a magazine article advertising her wealth creation and educational seminars. We called her to have a meeting with us and found her to be gorgeous both inside and out. She had also done amazing things in her career and was credible; already wealthy in her own right at a very young age, so we knew she would be a perfect addition. It was important to us that each speaker and Read My Lips contributor walked their talk and Jodie was no exception.

All the women who have written in this book are everyday, ordinary women with husbands, children and houses to care for. Most of them work from home and have created their business as a result of a passion and a persistence that just will not quit. Some of the women have university degrees but most don't; they have educated themselves and become very successful in their own right. Too often we put too much importance on degrees and other qualifications but so often vision, life experience, passion and persistence are the keys to success. Every woman who has written in this book has invested time and energy into achieving their goals. None of us can be found lying on a lounge watching TV or reading a magazine throughout the day, we know there are only 24 hours a day and make the most of every minute.

Everyone has a want, but not everyone is prepared to get off their tush and do something about it. If you are someone who wants more but are not sure where to start, then this is the book for you. This book will inspire, motivate, and give you the skills you need to at least get started.

This is a beginning. This is not all of your learning. Once you have mastered the steps in this book then you need to educate yourself more on the particular skills you need in order to achieve the success you want. Never stop learning, but remember: you must act on your knowledge. Too many people get excited after reading a book or after going to a seminar and then do nothing about it. Make sure, by the end of this book, that you have made a 'self promise' – a commitment to yourself – that you will act on the wonderful knowledge you are about to learn. By acting on this knowledge I guarantee your life will be different. If you continue to do the same thing as you are doing now then you will continue to get the same results.

A foreword by Cyndi O'Meara...

For things to change, YOU must change. Insanity is doing the same thing and expecting a different result; don't be one of the insane people who live their life hypnotized by the media and living ordinary, mediocre lives, slinking through life just 'existing'. Get out there and start LIVING!

Decide now that you want more for your health, wealth, love and purpose for living. Thank you for wanting more for yourself, and for buying this book. Reach for the stars. Go for your dreams!

Read my (our) Lips and enjoy creating your new life!

Cyndi, Rachael, Kim, Fleur, Jodie & Allison.

What's on people's LIPS about Read my Lips:

'Anything this positive is good for everyone' Mary C

'Inspirational, Motivating, excellent straight-forward, practical information' Barbara C

'EVERY woman should do this seminar!' Felicity N

'A BIG thank you; it was simply the BEST!' Jill G

'Inspiring; it has given me more confidence to achieve my goals' Barbara T

'Fantastic, helpful information for everyone' Annie R

'I wish my daughter could have come' Trish P

'A fantastic opportunity to meet 4 great ladies who have helped me focus and want to change my future' Kylie C

'A wonderful group of women, I feel nervous with excitement that I have finally got it!' Leanne M

'Brilliant! Brought to mind my passions and an idea to research; reconfirmed my ability to achieve my goals' Anna K

'Excellent, highly motivating and encouraged me to live my dream and take control of my life, business and career' Anne J

'Attention to detail was excellent, great injection of positivity, easy to understand and has caused me to take action' Donna H

*Achieving your
LIFE goals*

Achieving Success, Learning The Art Of Conscious Creation.

> *'Success comes from doing the things others can't be bothered to do.'*
> Rachael Bermingham

If you *knew* you could create the life you've always wanted to and someone gave you the formula for achieving it, would you follow the process and do it? Surprisingly it is achievable by a process I call Conscious Creation. There are literally thousands doing it every day and anyone can do it but most don't because they find it too hard to start or to give it a go. So in this chapter, I plan to share with you *how* you can start and most importantly *how* you can achieve the success you desire.

Some of the wealthiest, most successful, and most *powerful* people of our day believe that by utilizing their conscious thoughts, feelings and actions in a very specific way, it can result in being able to live the life that most people only dream about. And from my humble experience I have to say – it is TRUE!!!

It may seem a bit 'out there', and as a *fairly* conservative person, even *I* am consistently (and pleasantly) surprised at what I've brought into my reality over the past 20 years by implementing some basic actions into my day-to-day life. People first laugh, then show amazement at the seminars I speak at when I share my story of consciously creating many fantastic people, situations and items in my life such as; my marvelous husband (yes my husband – can you believe it!!!!), my gorgeous son (and how perfect is he from the tip of his blonde curly head, to the tip of his cute little toes), business, wealth, income streams, friends, health, opportunities and even a free car!

So what exactly is Conscious Creation, why is it important AND how do you do it?!

Conscious Creation put simply is 'consciously creating your reality' and there are a multitude of ways in which to do this (in truth it could easily fill another book!). I'm going to touch on some of my favourites – the ones I use time and time again that seem to produce the desired results consistently for me and the people around me *and* that make you feel good at the same time. After all who needs to go the long way around things – let's *fast track*!

Firstly you'll need to begin by clearly understanding what it is *you* truly want.

You need to <u>know what you want</u> in order to receive it.

Due to the speed in which we live our lives now, we don't often (if ever) make time to stop and consider what we *really* love, want or wish for our lives to be like.

This in turn directs us to living *reactive* rather than *responsive* lives. When we 'react' to daily events with quick and reflexive habitual actions, there is little conscious thought involved and we therefore have outcomes that are usually the same over and over again. Now of course if you've developed great *positive* habits this won't be a problem – you will already be using your habitual reacting skills to the greater good of yourself and those around you, and life should be cruising along beautifully. But for most people, a stack of negative habits have been formed throughout their life span. These negative reactive habits, if left to foster and develop, often lead to more regular outbursts of: anger, jealousy, fear, anxiety, guilt, disappointment and the BIG dangerous one: depression. Regardless – all of these will not only make you feel terrible, they will hinder you in living the life you really *truly* desire.

Understanding where you wish to be *and* what you want in life ultimately helps you in making quick, easy and *effective* decisions that are relevant and that will help keep you focused and steer you to the intended destination.

Often the thoughts, beliefs and perception of other people's lives can also distract us and lead us away from our own true desires, needs and path. We've probably all experienced 'the grass is greener on the other side' mentality.

As intelligent women; we all know by now that it's not a thought that serves us; all it does is takes our eye off *our* ball and onto someone else's life, a bit like watching a reality show really. Isn't your own life so much more interesting and exciting than watching or living someone else's?

Life success is determined by YOU and *you* alone. What would a successful and fulfilled life look like to *you* at the end of it? Asking this will help you gain clarity and focus on living that life.

Now you know what you want, it's time to live it ...well in your dreams firstly!

As the wonderful Walt Disney once said.....
'If you can dream it, you can do it'.

Dreaming is the second step in being able to consciously create what we want in life. It's also part of a 4 step process I've used since I was 16 that I've found to be a brilliant model for creating the life I had envisaged, as well as obtaining goals *and* drawing a host of sensational things into my life. The process is what I call:

Dream – Believe – Create – Succeed.

Day**dreaming** is imperative to creating a reality that you love, that you are comfortable with, that *excites* you, rings your bells, lights you up (as my friend Kim Morrison always says) and is basically the kind of life you enjoy living each and every day.

So how do you dream effectively?

The good news is - we *all* know how to dream, the key is in dreaming/daydreaming **productively** to achieve your dream life.

Sometimes we waste time dreaming ineffectively, such as daydreaming around a person or challenge that is upsetting you and entertaining thoughts of throttling them! Now *that*, even though it may help you feel temporarily released of pent-up emotion at the time, is *not* effective daydreaming and blocks good things coming into your life – in fact it does the opposite, it brings MORE of what you DON'T want into your life! Trust me I've experienced this too!

To **effectively** dream, you need to let your mind play with 'good and positive' visions of you having and doing the things you desire. By doing this you direct your focus to what you really *do* want, desire and love, which is imperative. The other key that is important in the dreaming step is to get into the *feeling* (by daydreaming) of what life would be like for you to have/do or experience something you REALLY want. 'Feeling' is a crucial part in the creation process. Our feelings are very powerful emotions and can work for us or against us. Whatever you put the most *feeling* into will manifest a whole lot quicker.

Daydreaming and getting into the feeling of doing the things that THRILL us enables us to make clearer, more relevant choices and decisions each day that are *productive* in helping us to move closer and closer to the things in life that *ring our bells*.

Effective Dreaming

This is where it can become a little tricky. Some people will *think* about doing it and won't get around to doing it, some people will *start* to do it and slowly forget more and more over the next few weeks, jigging around and procrastinating and *finally* some (hopefully YOU!) will be champions at it! The key thing to remember is this.... If you want to achieve something that has so far eluded you, then you MUST change the way you've gone about it in the past, otherwise you *will* get the same results over and over again. In order to achieve a different (successful) outcome you MUST do things differently. So if you are one of the people that usually thinks about it and then *doesn't* start, *or* you start *and then* stop – you already know (from previous experience) what your outcome will be – and *this* is the good news because you now know what *not* to do *if* you want a different result!

So to get started, please feel free to adapt the process I use. To start with all you will need is 15 minutes a day, as I said earlier – this will suffice. Choose a time of the day when you can dedicate this amount of time to creating a future that EXCITES you!!!!!! As a busy Mum, speaker and author, the best times I have for some un-interrupted peaceful mental time and space are first thing in the morning and last thing before I close my eyes at night this may work for you too, or maybe you'd like to try it in the shower, driving to work, going for a walk etc. It's not about doing it *one* particular way. Remember, it's about doing it successfully *your* way with a process that will help you get there a lot faster and with MORE clarity.

Each day **'invest in your future'** by spending a few moments each day contemplating the things we talked about previously that you *want* to see in your life, then go about the daydreaming or visualisation part of the process by seeing yourself living, having and experiencing it. Explore the *feeling* of it, do you like it, why, does it fit with who you really are? Are you proud to be living/doing/having it? Are you comfortable and more importantly are you feeling excited, even *ecstatic* about seeing yourself living/doing/having it? How has your life changed as a result of it? How has it impacted on others in a positive way? What else can you do now because you have it? How does it FEEL? Live it in as much detail as you can in your dream to ensure you feel every aspect of it.

This is such an enjoyable process when you start to do it. Not only is your mind consumed with happy thoughts, it helps you focus on what you DO want rather than what you DON'T want. You will be pleasantly surprised. The 'practice makes perfect' scenario comes to mind when you do this though. Sometimes old, ineffective and negative thoughts will threaten your process with sabotaging thoughts like 'I'll never get it', 'I don't deserve it', 'I'm not good enough', not smart enough, not pretty enough etc etc etc. Whatever you do, don't focus on these thoughts if they cheekily try to invade your 15 minutes of 'positive' creation time; instead simply dismiss the ineffective thought and replace it with positive thought to counteract it, while adding more emotion and energy around the thoughts and saying 'I AM deserving of this!', 'I AM well and truly on my way to achieving this and I am SO excited by it!' and let out some exciting enthusiasm at the end like a 'wooooooooooohoooooooooooo!!!!!!!!' After all if you don't get excited about the life you're creating no one else will!

Changing negative thoughts and reactions to positive ones is just like kicking any habit – you need to do it over and over again. Little bit by little bit, you will have fewer and fewer of the negative ones popping up and more and more of the positive ones popping up. You WILL master this if you keep at it. Let the clarity of what you want be your new motivation and focus for pushing aside those old, irrelevant and useless thoughts that have been hindering your journey to the life of your dreams!

Synchronize your head, heart and your beliefs to match.

To consciously bring something into reality, everything needs to be congruent, your head, your heart, your belief, your spirit -*everything* needs to point in the one direction, otherwise there is a conflict of interest and it will be next to impossible to achieve the desired outcome. I consulted with a lady years ago who wanted to be the Aussie Oprah, but during the dreaming process and my 300 questions, it soon became apparent there was a conflict of interest with her head and her heart. Her head wanted to be the Aussie Oprah, but her heart wanted a quieter life spending lots of time with the hunky husband she adored and her gorgeous little babies with a nice home and picket fence. So with this conflict happening she wouldn't have been able to achieve her goal – there would have been conflicts and challenges at every turn.

It's one thing to dream - I think we've covered just how to do this in a productive way, but what about *believing* you will achieve what you dream about into existence????

How to Believe

Step 2 in the Conscious Creation process is **believing** that you **will** achieve or create all that you **dream** of.

People find this step a little challenging initially, that is until they gain more insight into beliefs in general in addition to exploring their own beliefs. Throughout our lives we are literally bombarded with everyone else's *beliefs* about something. From religion, politics, how we should dress, act, think, be, look like, do, have, say, spend our time with, share with ohhhhhhhhhh the list just keeps going! Just think about it for a moment: most of the beliefs you grew up with aren't even those you decided on for yourself, they were handed down to you or taught to you. And like all good children most of us just went along with that. I did too until high school and then I started questioning why things were the way they were and a gazillion other things I was curious or confused about. This lead me on a very interesting journey and I learnt the most about myself I had ever learnt while doing so. The DREAM – BELIEVE – CREATE – SUCCEED process was born shortly afterwards due to the insights I discovered.

Belief is such an important part of who we are – it can be the driving force and instigator for accomplishing your dreams and on the flip side it can also literally cripple someone and prevent them from achieving even the smallest of goals.

Over the years we've seen and heard trillions of images, suggestions, and messages of doom and gloom. A normal day for some is a dose of D&G (doom and gloom) with the news report on the TV or radio, followed by another helping through the newspaper, and some more D&G throughout the day at work or listening to others, followed up with even more that evening during the night time news. How do you think that feeds our minds?

In workplaces and homes all around the world the topic of the day has increasingly shifted from something positive or inspiring to something negative, depressing and energy-lowering. Some TV commercials and programs condition us into thinking our normal attributes are not good enough. They tell us that we need to be taller, shorter, weigh more, weigh less, have more passion, be less busy, have this skin, that hair, this home, that car, stay at home with the kids, get out to work and earn a living, think less, do more….oh my gosh! No wonder people get soooooo confused, depressed and angry, and end up with a lack of confidence and direction – with someone telling you over and over in numerous different ways that you aren't any good the way you are right this minute –over time you're bound to believe it aren't you? I ask you this, without exploring *your* beliefs about what *YOU* really think, how can you know if the belief you have is real or relevant for you? Even more important to the Conscious Creation process is this: does each belief serve you or is it sabotaging you?

Start with writing out a list of big beliefs and then explore them. Do you really believe in them? Why? Do they help or hinder you? Knowing and understanding your beliefs is vital. If you have a thought like the one I used to have, which was, 'I don't deserve to be wealthy', then, it can literally keep you poor (it kept me poor for YEARS!). Every time I had money I'd sabotage myself in some way so I had an unexpected circumstance come up that would mean all my funds would be gone again.

You HAVE to change that belief so the path is free and clear of obstacles and all your dreaming work is not going to waste. You can dream day in, day out, and say all the affirmations in the world every day and none of them will manifest until you BELIEVE it will be. With this done, it's time to create some magic!

How to Create

By now most of us have heard the term 'The Law of Attraction', after all the first documentation of it, according to Wikipedia, was well over 4000 years ago!!!

But in case you missed it along the way, then you are going to LOVE this part because THIS is what *really* is going to fast track you to living the life you desire!

The Law of Attraction is this:
what you focus on most, you attract.

With that in mind, you can probably instantly see that if you are consistently worrying about lack of money, then you will attract more 'lack of money'. If you consistently think you are overweight, you will attract more things to happen for you to be more 'overweight' into your life. If you consistently think 'I'll never find the love of my life', you guessed it, you *will* never find the love of your life! My awakening around this came when I was sixteen years old (well over 20 years ago!) I was frustrated at what I *believed* at the time to be 'life' happening to me. I was feeling more and more inadequate, awkward, powerless, poor, unattractive and victimized by circumstances. In addition to that, the more it happened the more I focused on it and whinged and complained about it. I knew if my life was to change, then I had better start believing in myself and believing that I could have anything that I wanted.

I knew athletes, actors, musicians and business high-fliers had all been using the power of belief, attraction and visualization to their betterment, creating prosperous, successful, fulfilled lives for years, so at sixteen I started believing I could too. I used this Conscious Creation process haphazardly (I wasn't aware of the term Law Of Attraction back then) I was in the full swing of my teenage years so some things like boys, partying, shopping and friends often took over my better judgment to do it to the degree I do now! What I did start to notice fairly quickly though was that the outcomes of my creating were a direct mirror of the thoughts I was thinking, the words I was speaking, and the actions I was taking (on both ends of the scale).

The quantum physics behind this are now heavily documented and are incredibly interesting but far too extensive to go into in this book, given this area is only one part in one chapter, so I recommend seeking more information on this via three resources: The Secret Audio program (which the amazing Oprah Winfrey raved about on her TV show), a great book I came across called 'Excuse me your Life is Waiting for You' By June Grabhorn, and another more intensive read by Esther Hicks called 'Ask and it is Given'.

In a nutshell though, you (and your life) are mirroring EXACTLY what you have been focusing on. What you have been thinking, speaking and acting out is now occurring in your reality. So if you've been saying 'I'm sick and tired of having no money' then you're probably feeling tired and don't have enough money! Adds new meaning to life when you think about the quote 'you get what you ask for' doesn't it!

The best thing about this entire process is that you don't need to have a specialized skill, a university degree, be ultra intelligent, ultra fit, or ultra anything really *apart from* ultra motivated with a HUGE desire to live the life you really want. All it's going to take is a date with your mind each day – that's it!

Your mind and the power of your intention is at work every waking moment and all this time you've been using it to create your reality; mostly you just don't think about it – that's why I like to call this entire process (Dream, Believe, Create, Succeed) CONSCIOUSLY creating!

Only *YOU* have the 'make it happen' power to maximize the events and circumstances that occur for the benefit of your growth, happiness, health, prosperity and empowerment. The best way to do this is *consciously*. The more you think positive thoughts, take positive actions, and speak positive words and *FEEL* and *BELIEVE* them – then the quicker you are going to see great things start to happen in your world.

How to Succeed

Keep positive! To make this process work – you need to get rid of negative thoughts – they absolutely *must* go! They are hindering you more than you know, and let's face it, what good are they *really*? Do they make you feel good? There's no real point to thinking negatively other than experiencing it. The easiest way I found to decrease my negative thoughts was to simply replace them (counteract them) with a positive thought straight away, and when thinking that positive thought, I put as much *feeling* and *energy* into it as I can muster.

One of my biggies used to be 'I am sooooooooo tired!' – being a new Mum, parenting 11 days out of every 15 by myself (as hubby worked away), and running numerous businesses. I always felt exhausted! So many people used to say (still do) 'we don't know how you do it all' and it made me realize that I DID do *stacks* in my day, my energy levels were actually quite high (thanks to positive mental thought, good food and a goal focused outlook), so each time I found myself saying how tired I felt, I just said 'I have LOADS of energy to do everything I'd like to do today *and then* some!' It always left me smiling and feeling good and apart from that, I started to decrease the thought habit that wasn't serving me and I wasn't feeling wiped out by 10am either!

By picking out things and *concentrating* and *focusing* on what IS good, and what IS positive about the issue can certainly help you swing out of it. A good tip my husband (thankfully) taught me while nagging him about something one day, was: If you only focus on what's wrong then that's all you'll see. I'll admit I was not the most grateful person in the world, in fact I used to take most things for granted.

I have had to *learn* how to be grateful and it is one of the most important keys to living a happy life. Not only do you feel good when thinking of all the great things in your life, but it helps you focus on the positive AS WELL AS bringing more and more of the things you are grateful for into your existence. When you find yourself whinging, complaining, or berating someone else, choose one POSITIVE thing about the situation or the person, focus on it and be grateful for it. Keep thinking about this while exploring why you are grateful for it, and change the negative thought to a positive one.

Each morning see yourself having, doing and experiencing all your dreams. Get into the feeling of the sheer thrill of living life with these things part of your reality. KNOW that life is maneuvering to accommodate your new mentality around your desires and is bringing to you your order. EXPECT it, see yourself receiving it, getting excited about it, using it, celebrating it, doing it, being so so grateful for it – do this EVERY DAY as much as you can; the more you do it the quicker it will come.

Keep focused on this process. Like all habits – some take a bit of time to turn around, some will happen literally overnight. As I say in the seminars I speak at, this DOES take practice and concentration to do -but like everything you will master it and get better and better and *better* IF you focus and concentrate on it.

Apart from being grateful, CELEBRATE! Each good, positive, happy, exciting, prosperous, loving, feel-good thing that happens from the littlest thing such as a stranger smiling at you in passing to the biggest thing such as falling in love – CELEBRATE it!

This is also a way of showing appreciation and it says to your mind and spirit that you obviously like it so would like to draw more of the same experiences into your world. It's that Law Of Attraction in play – you *CAN* do it!

> *And as I always say –*
> **If it's meant to be, it's up to me!**

Becoming Your Authentic Self

> **'There is no one who does you like you do you'**
> *Rachael Bermingham*

I always say, 'Be yourself; there is no one who does *you* like you do you!' And it's true. No one else is more qualified to be you than you are, but like thousands of others, we've all tried to be someone else at one point in our lives.

Often we don't 'recognise' ourselves so we try to be the someone our parents, teachers or partners, or the media, want us to be.

Why?

After all, *we* know ourselves best. We know our strengths, weaknesses, inspiring and positive traits, and, yes, the less-than-attractive and even the negative ones too. We're all human and we were all born with natural talents, skills and gifts to use in our life. The point to our life is simply to do the best we can with what we have.

More often than not, the wheels fall off our life when we stray from *our own* path and try to be someone we're not. Or when we don't use, and even ignore, the natural abilities we have by pushing along in things that are not 'us' and doing things that we are constantly stuffing up, or that drain our energy or make us feel bad, sad or uncomfortable. This is nature's way of saying, 'Hello! Stop! You're not meant to be doing this'.

The point is, mostly people find it easier to keep doing what they've always done rather than looking inward and searching out what they really wish to do and be –finding their authentic (genuine, proceeding from the source, real) self.

Being your authentic self and walking your talk is no easy thing to do. It takes courage and conviction, both on a conscious and an unconscious level, to have the words you speak, the actions you take and the way you live your life congruent with your thoughts.

The first step to living authentically and acquiring instant personal integrity is to simply take responsibility for who you are, how you are, what you do, and why you do it. This is so amazing and surprising once taken on board. The very minute you assume responsibility for your thoughts, words and actions, you'll instantly feel empowered and have a wonderful sense of freedom.

Living a life that isn't you takes more energy and is more stressful than you realize until you've lived the authentic way. Taking back your personal power and being responsible for everything you do is incredibly liberating and feels like a huge weight has been lifted. For instance, if you are always running late, stressing and having to make excuses for being late, blaming it on your children, partner, friends or whatever, then you'll feel like you're on a roundabout of stress, always chasing your tail. But if you take responsibility, value yourself, fit in only what you know you can do within a single day and say no to everything else, leave for appointments 5 minutes earlier and leave a little room for breathing space between jobs throughout the day, your day will be a whole lot more pleasant. Not only will you not have to make excuses, you won't be feeling that stress welling up like a pressure cooker and exploding at the people you love, or sometimes at complete strangers! (Take a look at the Life Balance chapter on page 55 which talks about this in more detail).

After you've re-claimed your power and assumed responsibility for all that you do, say and think – the first BIG step – then work through the following pointers that enable you to move easily into living your authentic life.

LIPS Tips for Living Authentically

Listen to your heart and intuition. If you take quiet time (and yes, even we busy Mums can still find quiet time – after everyone goes to bed, before everyone wakes up, just prior to sleep and in the shower, for a few suggestions) to think/meditate/rest and listen to yourself. We all know when we've made a choice that feels right, as opposed to one that feels wrong; this feeling is your intuition. The more you practise doing this, the easier and more automatic it becomes. Your intuition is the clear, honest 'voice of your soul' and your mind is the voice of all the things you have learned during your lifetime whether they be accurate or inaccurate, so it's important to increase your awareness and practise 'listening' to your intuition.

Track your words; ensure they match your thoughts, feelings, beliefs and passions. Often we think one thing and say another, and this has come mostly from the way we were taught as we were growing up. We were taught to be polite, to not say anything that could be seen to be mean etc. and over the years we've put up with heaps of stuff to in order to 'do the right thing' and sadly, sacrificed our authentic selves in the process. There are many ways of 'speaking your truth' without hurting others and of course there is personal integrity to be taken into account, so with awareness we don't place ourselves in situations where we could be compromised in the first place.

Help others become empowered. Authentic communication is a learned art. In past generations communication was more effective as there were more opportunities for conversing. In today's world, there is little time to hang over the neighbour's fence to chat about life (if indeed you know your neighbors at all!) or engage in long chats over the dinner table with the extended family most nights. As a result, our communication has become less effective and we've gone from listening and letting others 'feel' out and discover their own solutions to troubles, to jumping straight into the deep end and providing a solution to the problem. What most people don't understand is this isn't authentic communication. In fact, this type of communication is more about you than the other person. Real, authentic communication is about allowing our mates to talk out and discover their own solutions. This allows them to be responsible for their own life issues and so become empowered. It also frees us from the pressure of having to solve their problems as well! The golden rule is to only give your opinion or advice when asked! Feedback is when you're *invited* to give your thoughts or comments; any feedback given without prior request is simply all about you and how you feel and is tagged as criticism.

Ask questions instead of giving answers where possible so that others find their own truth and direction. Provocative questions like; How can you make it happen, what do you need to make it happen, what is the best (or worst) thing that could happen, what concerns you (and why), how can I help, why is that so upsetting/important to you, how can you change it, can you change it, what is the first step you will need to take to having/doing/being it? These are just a start as the list is endless, but it you ask more questions of people, not only do you get to know them better, but they'll be lead to their own truth and you'll have been helpful in steering them there without judgment or another negative or compromising communication. What better friend could you be to them and yourself?

Be happy. Are you happy? If not, what will it take 'emotionally' to make you happy? We're not talking physically here with material items such as money, people etc. We're talking on a purely emotional level, finding out what YOU *need* to make yourself happy or happier. Being an intelligent person, you probably already know that no one or no thing can MAKE you happy. Happiness comes from within, so dig deep, start writing down some of life's pleasures that DO make you happy and ensure you do more of them (even scheduling in just one more item from your list each week will do wonders for your (happier) life). Then write out another list of things that would make you even happier – being healthier, getting more exercise to have more stamina, resting more, and laughing more. –Once you have this list, set about introducing actions into your day to make them happen. Remember, what you focus on most becomes your reality, so incorporating things that you love, or that make you happy into your life, lifts your spirit.

✐ **Get over yourself!** I'm saying this in the kindest way, and the reason is that sometimes we get a little too consumed with ourselves, with the whole 'It's all about me' thing. Yes, honouring, respecting and loving yourself is extremely important; after all, if you're not complete, than how can you share and be a positive influence in others' lives? But I say it's all about us AND others. There's nothing less attractive than someone full of self-importance and nothing more attractive than someone genuinely and generously helping others. So maybe it's time to think about what you can do to help your family and friends and others in the community. How can you make a positive difference in someone's life today?

✐ **Examine your beliefs.** Surprisingly, we grow up with a host of beliefs that, when you think about it, are mostly someone else's! Think for a moment; your ideas about religion, politics, life, relationships, nature, food, and money all stemmed from the people you grew up with, your education and the events you experienced or witnessed. Now we all know that our lives evolve and we grow, and so do our beliefs; the more educated we become the more our idea of the world around us changes and evolves too. When I examined my beliefs, I was floored by how many really didn't matter that much to me, didn't 'feel' right, or, worse, I actually didn't believe in at all! Write a list right now of some of the beliefs you have down one side of a page, ponder on each one and start crossing out the ones that you don't really 'feel' are your beliefs anymore. Create your own list

to show how YOU feel. Beliefs are amazing; not only do we have our personal beliefs, but we also have cultural beliefs thrown in as well! In the western world, blowing your nose in public is a fairly natural thing to do, but in some Asian countries the belief is that it is a rude gesture. There's no right or wrong here of course, it just is; it's whatever you decide it to be. So why not sort out the beliefs you have, and unclutter your mind. Let go of guilt and attachments. As I say, you are not your past; your past is a compilation of experiences.

Question yourself. Every time you get angry, upset or have an emotion that feels uncomfortable, start asking yourself what is provoking this emotion in you, and why? In this way you learn more about yourself and can grow out of the limitations of things that create challenges and problems for you or don't serve you. Understand you have a choice as to how you react to everything. Be crystal clear on what the emotion is and continue to ask yourself 'why' you are feeling like that until you hit the truth behind the emotion; only then will you know it, and be able to move out of it. Another great way to move on from old limitations is to look at them from a different angle or perspective to see if that truth feels more right for you. Change the perception of the event or circumstance and engage in thoughts about it from that new mindset.

Know what makes your heart sing. Everyone has a purpose, what's yours? If you have a job or career that doesn't make you feel excited or happy, then you're not putting your true talents, skills and passions to work. They're still hibernating or being ignored and you need to pull them out and use them. Write your passion list (see chapter on Creating an Income from Home) and find out what you can use to not only help others' lives become easier and happier, but be income-producing for you too.

Value, appreciate and take care of yourself. By doing this you become naturally optimistic, honest, healthy in mind and spirit, more energetic, confident, powerful, generous, loving and authentic to who you are.

Tune in – not out; listen to the Universe/Spirit/God/Love – there are signs everywhere out there. Get back to nature as much as you can

– a walk in the morning to clear your head and be ready for your day; a swim in the ocean or creek floating on your back and just listening to yourself (I LOVE doing this, it's one of my favourite things!); lying out in the backyard on a towel under some shade listening to the birds and the world around you; walking through a rainforest or trekking up a mountain. Take a moment and commit to doing some activity involving nature this weekend, it helps you stay grounded and in tune with your inner voice.

Live authentically. It is one of the most precious gifts you can give to yourself. It increases your vitality, you feel lighter (not having to carry the heavy luggage of manufactured emotion on your back), it shows you how you value, respect, appreciate and love yourself for you; and, it's incredibly rewarding and a whole heap more peaceful!

And lastly, be patient in stepping into your authenticity. It takes time and effort to change the way you think and get back to who you really are. For some it's been years since they've lived an authentic life, (even back to when they were babies!) so during the process, surround yourself with inspiring, positive, loving, supportive people who truly love you and enjoy seeing you shine in all your natural, authentic brilliance!

Remember we are forever organic, be prepared to change your self perspective to complement your growing and evolving self.

Who Am I, Who Are You?
Personality Profiling

Understanding what makes us all 'tick'
Allison Mooney

> *"First we must know who we are then we can understand others, which enables us to relate better."*
> Florence Littauer

For well over two decades now I have been fascinated with understanding what makes people tick. No, I am not 20 years old. It seems that I am just a slow learner as it took the two decades in my marriage to finally figure out that my wonderful husband sees the world so differently. Could it have something to do with the way we are wired?

Those 20 years in the marriage flew by like it was yesterday. Life was mainly involved with the growing and developing of our children. I loved that time so much; mothering really fitted with me.

Now I was entering into a new phase: that empty nest period; although mine was not an empty nest of the home, but of the heart – and emotions. While the girls weren't around as much, I was working out of the home with my husband running a community programme for young kids, trying to stay fit, socialising and dealing with all the demands that come at us through living. I never thought much about how we were wired.

It seemed I was on a ride, and it was getting faster and faster.

But I was 'Superwoman' – every hard-working woman knows the ride – and Superwoman sometimes crashes. (They never tell you that in the movies though!!) Mind you, I'm glad she did because I found some insight that liberated me and set me on another path – a path I never would have imagined and a ride I am so enjoying, even now at 59 years of age and still married to the same wonderful man.

I remember that night so clearly. I was phaffed out – lying on the couch after having my run, making dinner, ironing and planning the next day. What did I have to give to my man at the end of the day?

I looked up at this special man who had happily been sitting on the couch after dinner setting himself up for a good night's telly. Of course he would never miss the news and the sports. Tape the sport; watch it; replay it. Generally contented to do the mundane 'day-in-and-day-out', his reward had come. He had worked hard all day for this window of pleasure.

Why did I not share his interest? How different we were! I love variety, flexibility, and the thrill of taking a risk while my husband loves structure, no stress, planning and security. Why could I so quickly abandon the stay-at-home nights when a girlfriend phoned and wanted to meet me for a coffee somewhere? And why was it so important for my husband to finish seeing the news or completing a task before focusing on something else, or even considering some social event, especially after sundown. Of course he couldn't play until everything was finished. (It may be the opposite for you. You may love the stay-at-home nights, while your partner is planning the next social occasion.)

As I lay on this couch, the question I asked myself as my head spun in this deep philosophical conversation warring within my heart was: "So how come we are attracted to someone so opposite?"

The answer came when an extraordinary, generous couple came to New Zealand from the USA. Florence and Fred Littauer have helped literally millions of people stay in their marriages and break down the walls of hostility around family and work colleagues. They gave me the tools for understanding this mystery of why we are attracted to someone so opposite.

Whilst we are unique and can be in a relationship with an opposite, we also can share similar personalities with others. That is what makes us instantly 'click' with some people (it seems as though they have been our friends for life) and yet others rub us up the wrong way – sometimes before they even open their mouth! Explained perhaps this way: Every day, the roads are filled with different people heading in different directions with different goals in mind, yet all of us drive smoothly along with few mishaps because we all understand some common laws: we stop at stop signs and red lights, we go on green, and we try to follow the speed limit.

In our relationships, both in the workplace and at home, we seem to have a few more bumps. "Oh yeah ... I've had a few of them." We wish we could straighten out all those other people – those very same people who want to straighten us out! "Really! ... Someone wants to do that to me?"

This simple tool, **Personality Profiling**©, is to communications and relationships what traffic laws and road maps are to driving – and I am so grateful I discovered it.

One thing we do know; there is no doubt that our relationships can be the most rewarding, and the most heartbreaking, aspects of our life! Regardless of your upbringing, circumstances or genetic predisposition, you were born with a temperament and raw material unique to you. Of course over time that has been moulded and shaped by occurrences in your life, but the 'personality (dominant) type' you were born with, is with you forever.

Personality Profiling© provides guidelines and directions which show us how to function individually and together; it gives insight into ourselves and those we are in contact with in a unique and simple way.

This knowledge, by the way, is not new. Hippocrates (2400 years ago) gave us insight into the theory of human behaviour. In a nutshell, he claimed we come pre-packaged with a particular frame of reference. About 60% of our personality is in our genes (the expression of the real you).I have two wonderful daughters, raised in the same home, but they couldn't be more different. Disciplined the same, same belief system, and yet so different. This might be the same for you. The traits can come from a grandparent or uncle or second cousin twice removed.

This chapter is not about the how to, but what to do with what we have. Identifying our dominant personality style helps us to work with our strengths and to maximise them, and also to identify the traits in us that are not so great and can irk others. The key is in not only being able to identify our own personality, but to understand how we are motivated, what our needs are, and what others need from us.

If we take a moment to understand who the other is and what motivates them and discover how to speak to them according to who they are, we will find both the workplace and the home will run with less friction and more productivity, respect will increase and everyone will find significance and value in what they do.

Imagine rekindling a marriage that feels like it is just meandering along, or bringing out the best in a child who seems to be going astray, or being a better boss who has the ability to increase your team's self esteem and productivity. Well, it is possible – and all with a little knowledge and understanding, and so much fun in the application! The richness of our relationships are measured best by how we communicate within them and communication is enhanced by modifying our behaviour and responses and being a mirror in the moment for those with whom we are communicating.

So let's do a mini-profile to find your dominant type. Remember, this is not about boxing people into categories or making people wrong. We are all different and this is simply a way to help us understand ourselves and others. As you delve into this you may find you are a combination of two or even three of the personality types. One of the four will speak more loudly to you than any other, particularly with regard to your emotional needs. That is your 'dominant' personality type. Ideally you are working towards understanding all four types, embracing each of their strengths and understanding their weaknesses.

Now without reading ahead (oh yes, there is one type that can't resist reading ahead!), look at the 4 groups below and choose the one that speaks predominantly to you.

Enthusiastic	Decisive
Talker	Loves to Lead
Funny	Strong-willed
Balanced	Thoughtful
Thoughtful	Fact-based
Patient	Persistent

For easy retention and application we'll use the following descriptions of the 4 dominant personality types (based on Florence and Fred Littauer's work) and give them names.

PLAYFUL
Enthusiastic
Talker
Funny

POWERFUL
Decisive
Loves to Lead
Strong-willed

PEACEFUL
Balanced
Thoughtful
Patient

PRECISE
Thoughtful
Fact-based
Persistent

To choose your dominant personality type here is a brief description of each one. Most often people are a blend of two, so for the sake of identifying them we will focus on each one individually.

If you chose the PLAYFUL type, your basic desire is to have fun. The **Playful** is identified visually by their stylish clothing, expressive gestures, smiling eyes, and loud voice.

The strength of the Playful is their ability to communicate. They love people; they are warm and very relational. They are so enthusiastic about everything you say and do. They talk a lot (they speak to hear their thoughts), and this can drive others crazy!

They especially like to be liked. Social acceptance and approval are vital to them. (A great fear for them is loss of social acceptance.) They are the most forgiving of all types. Why? Because they don't remember yesterday! Most often they don't carry grudges.

They stay motivated because of their ability to focus on today and tomorrow; they're always planning the next social event. They are loud and their gestures are strong and expressive. They love to touch and that can get them into a lot of trouble as well. Because of their loudness they have huge belly laughs. Their motto is: 'Life is to be enjoyed, so get a life.' Playfuls bring great energy and innovation to a team as they are very creative.

Now there is a down side! This is when their strengths are out of balance and pushed to the extreme. One weakness that Playfuls struggle with is that it takes effort to be organised. They can learn to be organised but it sure takes energy. They often sacrifice 'back-end-delivery' for 'front-end-approval'. Left to their own devices they can be hugely messy; their handbags, cars, workstations, wardrobes and drawers are places the Precise types stay well clear of as they find it difficult to be in environments such as this.

There is a dichotomy here where Playfuls will have a meticulous office or home where others can see, for social approval, but the hidden areas reveal the true Playful. They're great starters but are so easily distracted that projects and tasks are often not finished.

> *A Playful wife was berated by her Precise husband. "Finish what you start. You will find a sense of order in your life when you do!" She looked around the house to see all the things she had started but hadn't finished. So, before leaving the house that morning, she finished off a bottle of red wine, a bottle of white wine, the Baileys, the Prozac, some Valium, the rest of the cheesecake and half a box of chocolates!!!*

Playfuls don't intend to irritate others by being this way; it's just that they would rather be with people and enjoying their company, than organising these areas.

They are great storytellers, but can tell stories at the expense of truth. They just love having an audience, and if they can make the story more interesting with a little embellishment, so be it. In a social setting you often hear them say: "That's enough about me, let's talk about you," but it doesn't take long before the conversation is back to them, or a story about what happened to them. They have no secrets. They talk as if it's their last night on earth!

They're not given to detail. These are the ones you will find wandering aimlessly around multi-storey car parks, looking for their car at the end of a working day. When they leave their car in the morning, they just don't think about where they are, or notice where they've parked. In fact, they just get a sniff of the shops – oh how they love the stores – and they're gone.

One day when I had been in the city I returned to the car park to find my car missing. I rang my Precise/Peaceful husband; I knew he would have a solution for me. He asked me a lot of questions, as most Precise do, before proceeding. "Did you take note of where you left the car? In fact where you are standing now, have you noticed the pillars that are holding up the next storey? Do you see numbers and letters on those pillars?" His tone of voice changed here and it became terse and reprimanding. He said, **"They're written for people like you!"** Playfuls do not notice details so I was totally unaware of those letters and numbers!

Playfuls also wilt under criticism and poor reviews, so if you have a Playful in your life, always commend them. Commend, recommend a course of action, then commend and commend again if you are coaching them in any way. Given encouragement they absolutely thrive. They love flexibility and a variety of tasks; if left at one task day in and day out, they lose motivation. They are great starters, but find finishing difficult; they're easily distracted. They're also usually time-poor because they over commit themselves.

It's easy to spot Playful children. They are the ones who charm you into doing things.

> *"Daddy, come out and play with me," the boy says.*
> *Daddy goes out into the garden and says,*
> *"OK what shall we do?"*
> *"Oh Daddy," says the boy. "I'll throw the*
> *ball and you shout wonderful."*

It's all about them!

So what is it that Playfuls need?

You will motivate Playfuls by giving them:

- Attention
- Affection
- Approval
- Acceptance

Sometimes you'll wonder why you should give so much to these types, but if you don't shower them with these gifts, they will go looking for someone who will. You can be a wonderful leader and have great influence if you know what others want and try to meet their needs.

If you chose the Precise type, your basic desire is to get it right! Visually, Precise can be identified by their more classic look. They are meticulous in their dress favouring straight lines and dark, subtle colours. They are incredibly well-groomed and generally quieter, less demonstrative and more self-contained than the Playfuls. They like people, but they don't need them like Playfuls do, and they have a tendency to analyse everything. They're the ones who are kept together by hairspray and starch after coming through a storm.

They are fact and logic based. They love organisation. They ask themselves, "What is the expected result divided by the risk factor?" They have a fetish for accuracy. They are very rational and are more objective in their thinking and always think before they speak. They find it difficult to understand emotional concepts but they're great planners (good money handlers). They want to know the down side – to all that will go wrong.

They see a problem and just want to fix it. Be careful if your partner is a Precise because if you go to the bathroom in the middle of the night, you might get back and find the bed made! They love order and get depressed when there are too many mistakes.

I didn't know until I married a Precise that there was a right way to put a toilet roll on a toilet roll holder. Yes, you Precise will be nodding right now. I now know it goes up and over, right? Then you don't have to go looking for it. Expect to hear: "Did you put the lid on properly? Is it put back in the right place?"

Interestingly, unless we understand these differences we can quickly be offended by those we come in contact with, work with, or even live with.

When we realise that what irritates us about others (their weaknesses!) is everything that we are not, we often become more tolerant and patient with them. In fact, when you understand this, you respect those who are different. Remember: different, but not wrong.

"Work before play" is what the Precise live by.

A Playful wife comes home after a hard day's work excited over the success of her day. She throws her arms around her husband and says, "Let's have a cuddle in the lounge before dinner." He pushes her away, "No I have to mow the lawns first, and then we will."

Work before play is so important for the Precise types! They can't relax until their jobs are completed and it's interesting to note that when they are upset, they'll get into the cleaning mode. They'll clean vigorously, anything, while stewing over the issue. When they are upset, they won't say anything; they'll throw you into a guessing game, but their body language gives them away. That look of disapproval, the tch-tch muttering that goes on under their breath!

They abhor making mistakes, and are hard on themselves. If you were to compliment them over something they did, they would already have had the post mortem on the situation and let you know how they could have done better in such and such an area.

They have high ideals and get disappointed in others when they don't see them do things with excellence. They can make others feel less intelligent or less than competent.

They have brilliant minds and appreciate the arts and music more than any other type. They thrive on seeking knowledge and are drawn to specialist areas such as medicine and engineering. Aren't you glad about that? Who else would take the rigours of Medical School and then specialise for another seven years. They go the long haul. Can you imagine a Playful surgeon operating on you? They'd find an organ after they have sewn you up, and think, "Oh dear, where did that come from? Oh well, never mind!"

Precise types carry and write lists for everything. They have lists waiting to go on lists. They get great satisfaction from working through these lists as well.

You can quickly pick a Precise as they communicate. They love to give you information in complete, and consecutive, order. If you were to ask how their day went, they would proceed to say:

It started at 6.42am when the alarm went off. I got out of bed and opened the drapes. There was the most amazing sunrise. The sun was vivid red, and was reflecting itself in the Monkey apple tree. There I saw a wood pigeon. It was huge, and as I observed it I was curious to know its Maori name...

That took about five minutes, but they need to tell it all so you get the full picture. You can be standing for half an hour waiting to hear how their day went.

Sometimes in a relationship you may feel the Precise don't trust you as they are constantly asking a heap of questions like: "Where are you going? How long are you going to be away? When are you coming home? Who will you be with?" This could so easily be misinterpreted, but it's just that they want the full picture. In order to speak and communicate well with the Precise it is so important that you give them ALL the information.

Precise serve tirelessly in Third World countries. They care deeply for our planet. They appreciate our world, and stand up for moral justice and integrity.

Because their leadership style is strategic, their critical skills work for them. They know how to get from 'a' to 'b' and can see the pros and cons in every situation. They have a tendency to say 'no' before 'yes' which can upset others.

In an email, a Precise described a picture of some ducks he'd sent as an attachment:

> *Each year around this time (almost like clockwork) I've happened to spot a pair of ducks (male and female) stopping off in our pool on their migration. I've only seen them one day each year and only for a few minutes so I've been lucky to spot them each year. I suppose they could come some other day but I doubt it. I know the times because the photos on my digital camera retain the 'time taken' properly.*

> *I'm not sure if they are the identical pair but I suspect they are. Interesting that they choose to use our pool; normally there is water on the winter blanket. This year we had to drain the pool to have the liner repaired and it was totally empty until we had about 7 days of rain collected in the bottom – just in time for their return. Sometimes nature can be quite amazing – even in the city.*

Listening to what people say and how they say or write it gives you a clue to who they are ... as expressed *Precisely* above.

To reach and motivate Precise, be aware of what they desperately need:

- Sensitivity to their feelings
- Space to be alone
- Silence – no people sometimes
- Support when they're down

They don't mind being alone; they restore their soul that way.

If you chose the Powerful type, your basic desire is to have control. Powerfuls can be identified by the energy (or sometimes tension) they bring into a room. They're often seen with an intense look of concentration (sometimes frown or a terse look) but they're not angry, just focused; they have a lot going on in their minds and can be perceived a someone who needs to be given a wide berth.

They are functional dressers, wearing clothes that won't restrict them; they are not 'frou-frou' but wear strong and powerful colours.

They are strong Visionarys, focussing on the future, They're big picture types. The see the world of possibilities, and go for them. There is no-one quite like the Powerful to achieve. They are 'doers'. Have a high achievement drive, ambitious, goal driven and very decisive. They move quickly and exist to bring change. They have a natural instinct to physically demonstrate and produce. Therefore, have a inborn ability to lead, and are good at stepping up to the mark.

They are producers who can accomplish more in any given day than most and often find it difficult to rest. They work hard, play hard. Sleep interrupts their work! They don't want to work a 40-hour week, but a 40hour day. They have a tendency to be workaholic; in fact their greatest fear is sickness or loss of job. Why?

Because then they can't produce. They see this as loss of power. They were made to DO and their time frame is NOW!

Because they get the picture quickly, they are restless to the point that most meetings bore them, especially when they aren't at the helm. You can see them switch off and drift off to other thoughts and plans as other types talk around, look at the down side and go off on tangents. They don't really care if you don't like them. Its about productivity; they just want to get onto with achieving what their goals.

They like to do things themselves because they know it will be done and done quickly! Often, by default they pick things up because of the incompetence's of others that force them too.

They rise to the forefront in emergencies – they just love a huge challenge and normally excel in them! No test is needed for these types. Their conversation is bottom line: results. They are not only the Judge, but the Jury and the Executioner! Bumper stickers which can often depict the Powerful are:

Do not start with me, you will not win!

If you are not outraged, you're not paying attention.

Just do it!

If you manage Powerfuls too tightly, they'll tell you to "take your job and shove it."

Most often they are married to an opposite (Peaceful) and always want to know what their partner has done, whereas the Peacefuls have other needs – and it sure ain't productivity! The Peacefuls are laid-back and easy-going and don't have the frenetic drive that Powerfuls do. Before marriage we are attracted to an opposite, and if we don't understand the personalities, that truly can become a frustration.

Powerfuls need the Peacefuls to bring calm into their busy lives and I have often seen couples splitting because they view their spouse through a negative lens, rather than seeing what they do bring to the partnership. Remember: your weaknesses are simply strengths out of balance, or pushed to the extreme.

Powerfuls can view the Peacefuls as unproductive and lazy, and Peacefuls can negatively view the Powerfuls as pushy, demanding and controlling. The solution is to continually audit your thoughts to see how you are viewing the people you are relating to. If you are looking at their weaknesses rather than their strengths, then re-align by seeing the strengths they have and focus on them. Each personality type has different strengths and it's helpful to realise we need each type in our world.

To communicate with the Powerfuls one needs to speak in Readers Digest condensed version – short, to-the-point, logical. They love to talk bottom line and outcomes. They certainly don't waft with words and are very comfortable saying "Get to the point!" They're not afraid of confrontation, and don't care if you don't like them.

Powerfuls are easy to spot. They're usually pointing, telling 'some dummy' what to do. They're very restless people and when you're in their presence you can feel they want to move on. If you opened their minds, you'd find they have ten irons in the fire and are always searching for more to add to it.

This is the type that says: "I don't get ulcers! I give 'em!" They don't get mad; they get even. When you deal with them, it's not like a ball game where you get three strikes and you're out; its one strike only and you're out for life.

You can identify Powerfuls as children when you know what to look for. These ones show themselves early. They have leadership raring to come out. They can have poor peer relationships in the playground as they have a tendency to tell others what to do. Some Powerful children test their parents by pushing boundaries to the limit. They are very smart little people, but can drive their parents and teachers nuts.

To motivate and bring out the best in Powerful types give them:

- Credit for their abilities and accomplishments

- Appreciation for all they have done

- Loyalty in the ranks

If you chose the Peaceful type your basic desire is to have peace.

Peaceful types are identified by their casual, conservative clothes and fluid gestures.

Peacefuls are the 'salt of the earth' types. They are brilliant listeners, easy-going and balanced, the most balanced of all the four types. They love routine and are predictable and trustworthy.

They are conservers of energy "you never said it was a race!" These types are good Poker-players, never giving anything away. They have a wonderful dry wit with one-liners that have you in stitches – but they won't laugh with you; that takes too much energy.

They work best being motivated by rest as their reward. They think: "Why stand when you can sit, why sit when you can lie down?"

They'd rather be liked than right. They're hesitant to give an opinion as they don't like confrontation. They see a war going on and pull back; when the war is won, they join the winning team. They are very adaptable, and relational. They like people but, unlike the Populars, they prefer others to come to them.

When you have been in the presence of a Peaceful, you feel you have been sitting in a meadow on the hottest of days and had your feet soaking in a cool running stream. Their motto would be: "Why not put off today what can be done tomorrow."

They are well-liked and brilliant listeners, so others often confide in them and the Peaceful will bring clarity to any situation, putting things into context. (Intergrating the past, present and future) Their strength is bringing order out of chaos, and seeking harmony. They function systematically and efficiently. Great administrators and enjoy paper work and routine. They are very relaxed and pleasant people, making no demands to be in the limelight or pivotal positions of power. It's not to say they can't, but they would rather not. They can sometimes irritate others by not speaking up. They have things to say, but all too often the other types butt in and talk over them and never give these gems the opportunity to speak.

From a negative-lens view, Peacefuls bother others because they resist change and won't debate an argument, but they are now recognised to be the better Managers and Supervisors because of their non-abrasive ways and 'team support' leadership style. They have an incredible ability to bring clarity to the issues of the day. They genuinely listen without reproach, offering patience and tolerance of another's attitude and behaviour. They mediate well, and draw out others. They are diplomats and can stimulate discussion because of their ability to look out for others. They can easily build a team around them where they know they are lacking; i.e. they bring in the visionaries, the decision-makers, and the strategists. Peacefuls are the ones who do that best – creating harmony in any situation.

The way to motivate Peacefuls is through:

- Respect
- Valuing who they are, not what they do
- Lack of stress
- Peace and quiet

A Closer Look at The 4 Types

Each personality type asks certain questions that they relate to the best:

> **Playfuls** ask **Who?** – They focus on people
> **Powerfuls** ask **What** or **When?** – They focus on results
> **Precise** ask **How?** – They focus on facts
> **Peacefuls** ask **Why?** – They focus on reasons

It's interesting that so often we operate only from where we stand, instead of taking the time to really look at the different people we come in contact with and how we can bring out the best in them by speaking to their needs and motivations – not from our own.

As mentioned earlier, in relationships we are mostly attracted to an opposite in personality. A Fun type will be attracted to a more Organised type while the Leader type is more drawn to the Follower – this brings balance for them both.

People often comment: "We're so different, the only thing we have in common is that we got married on the same day!" And this seems to give them a licence to bale out of the relationship. If only we took the time to see how these differences could work for us, rather than against us.

When working with others it's important we gather all types around us to get a more balanced perspective.

It's valuable to have all four types around us, but what usually happens over time, as it does in relationships when pressures occur, and timeframes are in place with deadlines fast approaching, we start working out of our weaknesses. We then start looking at each other from that negative-lens view, causing frustration which results in conflict which then brings huge tensions where we work or even at home for that matter. Productivity decreases and relationships break down, and then we get into trouble because we go looking for our own kind. (Now that is a whole other chapter!)

We often view the Personality types in a certain way, seeing the:

Playful as phoney, insincere, unreliable
Powerfuls as insensitive, intolerant and demanding
Precise as dull, picky and boring
Peacefuls as gushy, spineless, wishy-washy and stubborn

It is well documented that one of the main reasons people choose to get out of relationships or leave where they work is because they do not feel valued. Understanding and applying this simple tool can really save a lot of heartache, and expense. Let your partners, and co-workers (and children) know they are valued.

When we simply take a step back and focus on the people we have in our lives and workplaces, celebrate their differences and speak to them according to their needs, a transformation takes place, and productivity increases.

The different personality types have different qualities and strengths:

Playfuls are optimistic and expressive, and they bring creativity, energy and innovation

Powerfuls love to work, they're natural born leaders and they bring vision, focus and assertiveness

Peacefuls are easy-going and adaptable, cooperative and pleasant, and they add diplomacy, clarity and harmony

Precise organise well, function well alone, and are strategists who bring method, structure and quality

If we take a moment to understand who the other person is and what motivates them and speak to them according to their personality type, there will be less friction in our lives, everyone will find significance and value in what they do, productivity will increase, and everyone will be a winner.

Personality Profiling© is a wonderful tool to help you identify others so you can speak to them according to who they are and impact them positively because you understand them.

For example, when speaking to a:

PLAYFUL – Tell them stories; give colourful details; give acceptance; give attention; give approval for their very being; don't tune out.

POWERFUL – Keep communication short and to the point; give appreciation for their achievements; give the bottom line first; give sound bites then allow room for them to jump in; give supporting detail only if asked or it's critical; accept curtness (they are not rude … just project focused).

PRECISE – Ask them if it is a good time to talk; don't interrupt activities or communication; respect time/space/silence/schedule – don't pry; give factual, orderly details, not chit-chat; laugh and cry with them – don't try to jolly them up; prepare – think through what you will say.

PEACEFUL – Show respect and look for the positive; give a few choices; freely give praise; learn to say: "I appreciate your …" (attribute); give focused attention; wait to speak until they're completely finished.

This understanding has worked for many people in relationships and in marriage. Learning to fill each other's emotional tank is the key. It's natural for us to speak from where we sit. The challenge is to pick this up and risk speaking to others **according to who they are**.

When I started giving my husband what he needed as a Peaceful/Precise, a shift happened. He listened more and gave more; he became more outgoing, more like the person he was designed to be. And not only my husband responded; friends and family, clients and customers did as well. This is a very powerful tool that can help us connect better to others. There have been thousands of people who have taken the time to learn about and apply the principles around personalities and their relationships have benefited hugely.

A couple of years ago at an airport bookstore, I noticed a magazine with a headline: Married to a Man with No Ambition – Unambitious Husbands, Ambitious Wives. Curious, I purchased the magazine, and the article was centred on 'go-getter' type women. Women who find it hard to relax, who love to achieve and climb quickly up the corporate ladder only to find they seem to be attracted to, and marry, partners who are the laid-back, salt-of-the-earth types.

I responded to the article in a Letter to the Editor:...

> *Whilst I agree in part with the article, I would like your readers to take a step back and perhaps consider how personality types impact on relationships. By doing this we can understand people better and what motivates them. The most important thing we can get out of this is: Different, but NOT WRONG; just different.*

It wasn't difficult to detect the Powerful personality in the various women the writer described. One dead-give-away is the description of their partners as described in the article. They are usually attracted to the Peaceful types. (And don't we need a Peaceful in the world of these women to bring tranquility and balance!)

While it can drive these Powerful women nuts, they can overlook how important the Peaceful personality is in their life. Usually the frustration comes when each is not speaking to the other's need and consequently they have unexpressed, unmet needs, as was the case with those women in the article.

The women described in the article are productive, high achievers, and natural-born leaders; they are extroverts, decisive, quick and active. Because they fear being sick and unable to work, you can understand why they have a passion to produce.

They are more task-oriented, than the Peacefuls. These Peacefuls are relational; they want peace at any price. They have no need for recognition of what they've done; they want to be respected and valued for who they are!

This can be so helpful in a relationship when we learn to communicate to their personality not from our own.

So often we can look at a personality and think, "Oh I wish I had their ability to be such-n-such ..." but fail to see that each personality has qualities and strengths that the others don't have. We can spend endless hours and much energy trying to do what we're not naturally good at. Success comes when we focus on what we do well and operate from that stance.

Or they say, "I wish I was married to the same type." Well some are, but they have to work a little harder in their relationship. The relationship can work, but one has to be aware of the pitfalls.

Can you imagine two Powerfuls in the home? Both busting to get out there and achieve; both wanting to take control. Oh my there'd be a few sparks in that relationship as each strives to take control. These people think: "Do things my way NOW."

What about two Precise in the home. They are thoughtful, cautious creative and analytical, and excellent at details, but their strengths can be their very weakness. They have a tendency to want it 'perfect' all the time, which puts a great strain on a relationship. They are always thinking, "If it's worth doing, it's worth doing right! Pity help you if you put the toilet roll on the toilet roll holder incorrectly!

Precise need the opposite Playful type. These people are the fun loving. They're energised by others and avoid monotony. They live in the present. They're boisterous and love to use their humour to lighten serious situations. They work to a minimum and just love fun and frivolity. You can see why they would need an opposite in their life.

Just imagine two Playfuls in a relationship – party, party, party, with no systems and a rather chaotic home. They mean well, but tasks are secondary. They are great starters, but not good finishers because they get distracted.

Precise love sorting these Playfuls out! The relationship goes wrong when they fail to understand the different needs of each type, and think that organising them, insisting that they should spend time out reflecting and enjoying the depths of life is the way to go.

This is not what energises and motivates Playfuls. Give them a shopping mall or a group of people where they can tell their latest stories, at the expense of truth of course (they're given to exaggeration).

The two Peacefuls in a relationship have to work hard at getting going. They love people, but they wait for people to come to them. They have this dry wit that has you on the floor absolutely doubled over in laughter at their one-liners, but wouldn't join in the hilarity. (That takes energy!) They're not great initiators. Remember, rest at the end of the day is their motivation. They control by procrastination, which absolutely drives the Powerful nuts; but take these people out of the world, and we'd have no peace – believe me!

I would say the Powerful women find relationships the most challenging, and I guess a Powerful man possibly would find the relationship having the same issues. But on the other hand, if the Powerfuls could see the benefits of a Peaceful partner in their life, absorbing all the tension and energy that flies in the door at night and bringing a sense of quiet and calm in the storms of life, the Powerful might appreciate and value this tremendous asset they have in their life. I say asset, as the Powerful measures life in achievement and results.

Please Powerfuls, if you have a Peaceful partner, remind yourself they are not out to get you with their un-abrasive, unmotivated, stance; they want to add to your life by creating an environment where you (the Powerful) can hear your thoughts – Yes, the Peacefuls are wonderful listeners – and then weigh up the unfinished business and get on with it when they are ready to get on with it. There are many more examples like this – but that's another book on its own! .....

So, all the best to you 'ambitious mismatches' – take a step back and look from another perspective; you see, there are three other perspectives as well as yours!!

In business everyone is trying to define leadership.

It's influence; nothing more, nothing less. Influence according to people's personality. People respond to those who are interested in them, so speak into their 'tank' and you will see dramatic improvements in the relationship.

A really wise person once said: "The greatest good that we can do for others is not to reveal our riches to them, but theirs to them." There is so much potential locked up inside people and you can help them discover it. Go! Dare to be different! Dare to be the extraordinary leader who influences.

> **Bring out the best in those you encounter – according to who they are.**

Life Balance
Time Management

> '*We all have 24 hours in a day, it's how you use it that will determine your success*'
> *Rachael Bermingham*

Time. It's one of the few things we were all born with that was dished out evenly. We were ALL given 24 hours in a single day, no more, no less. But listening to others it would seem this isn't the case. Some say they never have time for anything; work, to see friends, family, to exercise, go grocery shopping, call a loved one for their birthday, arrive on time, to do ANYTHING other than their day to day tasks – they seem to be incredibly busy (even chaotic) but it doesn't look like they've done much at all sometimes. Yet others fit in all of this and a gazillion other things and still get sleep, are relaxed and balanced. So what is the story?

In a nutshell (and to cut to the chase and save you time!) it all comes down to how we manage our day. For some it comes naturally and for others (like me), well, let's just say we need to learn how to do it. If you're not an organized person as you read this – there are 2 (main) reasons. 1/ It's not a priority for you – you don't have anything in particular that requires you to feel like you need to be organized, or 2/ You do want to know how to get more time back in your day to do the things you want to do rather than HAVE to do BUT just don't know how.

I was in the first category right up till 8 years ago when I did have a reason to get organized… I've always been an entrepreneurial woman who has the desire to do many things in my life, but not being organized meant that I constantly felt overwhelmed and far too busy to put any of my ideas into action. One day my desire to succeed at one of them, a few of them, in fact to action ALL of my ideas simply grew far to great to waste any more time on just existing – it was time to LIVE and put some effort into making my dreams come true and to stop making excuses.

If you're reading this book now, there's a better than average chance you too have a burning desire to achieve your goals otherwise you would not have bought/received Read My Lips. From experience, I know by learning, practicing and implementing these strategies they WILL serve you extremely well in helping you to not only claw back precious time in your day, but also in helping you to become more focused directing you to your goal destination in super quick time. With the following tips, you gain the benefit of my experience without having to spend two years of your life learning it and without outlaying $3000, both of which I did, and in truth would do again in a heartbeat – it really is SOOOOOOOOO worth it. Even though challenging initially I do credit my successful life balance to the effective time management skills I have learnt which are a key ingredient to achieving all I have achieved.

In the past three years, I've had a gorgeous baby boy Jaxson, co wrote my first book (Read My Lips) while breastfeeding him, co wrote my second book (4 Ingredients which has now sold over 700,000 copies) during his day sleeps, and co wrote my third book (4 Ingredients 2) during his four hours of kindy each week and when he sleeps at night. I'm now writing my forth book (which I've been writing for four years now) a marketing book due out in 2009. In addition to this I also solo run my speaking business, co run Sunshine Coast Speakers a booking bureau for inspiring, informing and entertaining speakers who reside on the Sunshine Coast with Cyndi, co run 4 Ingredients with my beautiful life-long friend Kim, and am a hands on Mum and do the normal weekly tasks like cooking, cleaning, groceries, washing, exercise etc. It HAS taken a bit of practice (and still does) to learn to say no and be more ruthless with my time but I can tell you now –

Life Balance Time Management

I wouldn't haven't been able to fit in anywhere near this amount of activity and still have time to film my TV show with Kim, do stacks of interviews, appearances and flights here, there, and everywhere!

It doesn't matter who you are, what your family circumstances are, we are ALL busy. It's just working out how to maximise that 24 hour period so it works for you rather than it working against you. So I thought I'd share some of my tips, from one busy person to another busy person YOU, I hope they are as helpful to you as they have been to me.

LIPS Tips for managing your time.

GET A DIARY OR SCHEDULE. This is not only a *FANTASTIC* resource for managing your time, but it also helps you to remember everything important *and* allows you to see what you have in your day already so you don't over commit. It also helps you work to your character style. I always say we come in **3 different varieties** – the **hero** who has to be responsible and take control of everything and everyone so things get done etc... the **people pleaser** – says yes to everything so they don't have to offend anyone by saying no, and the **lounge lover** – the person who is either finding it hard to get started simply because they don't know how or because they simply don't want to. Regardless of your character we all aspire to do things and having a schedule to work from assists us to help make this happen.

PLAN. This is *incredibly* essential. Spend some time planning what you want to do so you know *what* steps you need to take and *when*. This helps you tenfold to achieve any goal you desire. I sit down once a month and begin adding appointments to my schedule. I start with everything to do with my family and friends (as that is my 1st priority), so birthdays, anniversaries, special events and holidays go in so I don't forget the most important days to the special people in my life. If your schedule reflects more of what your want to rather than what you have to do then you will always feel good; doing the opposite will make you feel unhappy. Then I add to my schedule all my trips, speaking engagements, and appearances and meetings, next comes the things that need to be done *but* are flexible in terms of when I can do them such as exercise, catch ups with friends, groceries and my favourite (not) cleaning house.

Life Balance Time Management

🌿 **WORK OUT YOUR OWN STYLE.** Not everyone has the same amount of energy and we all work better at various times throughout the day. So if you're an early-bird, schedule in as much work in the mornings as possible as this is when you will be at your most productive and effective. If you're a night owl – do it during the evening hours. This will also depend on your responsibilities too, my day pre-children looked a whole lot different to what it does today after having a baby. Before Jaxson I could book something in and allocate it to a time slot ie; 7.30-8.30am check emails, 8.30-9.30 business calls, 9.30-10.30 marketing consulting with Jane etc etc. These days I put 5 things in my day schedule and I do them when I can. Having children means you can't always stick to scheduled times so I alleviate the stress by putting the five activities into my schedule and make sure I do them at some point throughout the day unless it's a meeting or speaking engagement which can't be moved around easily.

🌿 **USE A BUFFER ZONE.** We all have unexpected things that come up. Friends pop in, someone needed you to help them urgently, a job takes a little longer, transport is delayed, you slept in, or sometimes you just didn't feel like doing something that you had to do (which often masquerades the fact that you need to take a little time out!)... Each day wherever possible, make a space in your diary for a buffer zone so you still have another block of time to have another crack at finishing something. AND if you have finished everything, then you can relax and spend that time on YOU!

🌿 **OUTSOURCE WHAT YOU PROCRASTINATE ON.** We've all got our strengths – my weakness is in Myob data entry, so to alleviate any stress or costly mistakes at tax time, I have a bookkeeper who is simply *sensational* and *LOVES, LOVES, LOVES* doing it *and* does it incredibly well. I'm happy, she's happy and the tax man is happy so everyone wins and we're all doing the things we love rather than stressing over the ones we don't.

🌿 **MINIMISE UNECESSARY TASKS.** Before I *did* get myself organised, one thing you would find me doing CONSTANTLY was going to the supermarket every other day to get ingredients for dinner. Often it would be a costly trip because I'd go in without really thinking what we were having for dinner so would end up with a variety of ingredients I didn't even get to use, and also waste time and fuel in doing it!

USE LISTS. An essential time saving resource is a shopping list. Ask everyone on a Sunday or Monday what they want for lunch and dinner the following week and put it onto a weekly menu list, extract the ingredients out of the recipes and put what you don't have in the cupboard or pantry onto your shopping list. This is a brilliant way of saving time and money. I would (of course) HIGHLY recommend my co-authored cookbook 4 Ingredients for saving time and money too!

USE COMPUTER TIME EFFECTIVELY. We've probably all been guilty of a little out of school internet surfing right? But it's one of THE biggest time zappers around. One site leads into another and another etc, before you know it 2 hours has slipped away from you. The other time zapper is emails. If you find yourself checking emails every 10 minutes or whiling away the hours in cyberspace, then a great tip I utilise is to allocate time for computer research and also emails and if you have to have your email open turn down the sound so you can't hear all those emails coming in.. I book a block of time for research and also check emails 1-2 times throughout the day; first thing in the morning and/or after Jaxson goes to sleep at night and only on my work days, never on weekends unless I've been away on holidays. This was really challenging to get used to, but it's sensational when you get the hang of it. You can fit far more into your day.

BE RESPECTFUL/RESPONSIBLE. Often people run late due to poor scheduling; however if you are consistently turning up late, this could be due to an emotional need of wanting to be thought of as more important or more valuable than the person you keep waiting. Is your being late a ploy to attract and receive attention, rather than a result of poor time management? If so, address your need and organize for this to happen in positive ways PLUS you're not stressing out and neither is anyone else – Happy Days!

🖋 DO WHAT YOU CAN THE NIGHT BEFORE. Sometimes I have to wake up at 4am in order to leave for the airport by 4.30am to catch a flight at 6am. I find it far more relaxing having as much as possible prepared the night before so I'm not rushing around like a crazy women. I iron my clothes, put everything including my bag, phone, laptop, suitcase, shoes, water bottle, fruit or fruit smoothie for breaky etc in the one area (usually somewhere on my way to the door) so I can jump out of bed, into the shower, get dressed and fly out the door. Everything that is in my trip pile goes (including sometimes a toy or two that Jaxson has thoughtfully added for me to take!). On a regular day - take the chaos out of the morning rush by preparing lunches, clothes and chores (like washing) etc the night before.

🖋 DELEGATE AND SHARE THE LOAD. If you have children, work with your partner or other parents to share school drop-offs and pick-ups. This is an easy way to give yourself more time and less stress in your day.

🖋 MEALS. Most of us don't enjoy cooking EVERY night, so give yourself a night off sometimes by cooking at double the quantity twice a week, and then freezing the second meal for a night when you simply don't want to cook, or if you have unexpected guests popping in.

🖋 BE RUTHLESS. I was always what I call a YES person, whenever someone asked me to do something I'd say 'YES! ', 'Sure, I'll do it!', 'No Worries!'. Howeeevvveerrrrrr this always left me highly over committed sacrificing time with the people I loved. So to alleviate that stress and so I don't put myself in such situations anymore – I use a diary/schedule which is a great tool for helping me to be ruthless with my time AND for not letting other things crept into my personal/family time. So when someone asks if I can do something I say sure let me check my schedule and I'll see when I can do it. If it's next week or in 5 months time I am comfortable about responding and KNOW that if my 24 hours is booked up, then it's booked up – if you work with it, it'll make life easier.

Not all of these things will work for you – but implementing as many as possible WILL assist things to run a whole lot smoother and if you allocate time and write down the things you want to do, you have 93% more chance in achieving your goals – now that's motivating isn't it?!

Life balancing does take some effort but it will repay you many times over in helping you create more time and income for yourself, as well as becoming a nicer less stressful person, having happier and more quality packed relationships etc etc etc

> *Time is our greatest commodity of all and something if wasted, you can never, ever replace.*

So managing our time is crucial to life, health and wealth success. We all have 24 hours in our day and it's what you do with yours that really counts.

Declutter (Lighten) Your Life

> **'Decluttering not only creates a void, but it also frees up energy and allows abundance to flow'**
> Cyndi O'Meara

Many years ago I picked up an amazing book on Feng Shui. While I didn't get too much into the mirrors and colours, although I found that fascinating, what I did really appreciate about the book was the decluttering aspect. The book basically said that if you have anything in your house, office, car, handbag or any other personal space that does not make you feel good – then get rid of it. That got me thinking.

I started to go around every room and cupboard in my house to see just how much stuff gave me no satisfaction, annoyed me or had no significance. There was a lot. So I made a promise to myself that I would clean out a room, and everything in that room, each week until the whole house was cleared. And so the grueling task began.

In the garage, there was no more car; in its place I put three boxes (which soon turned into three areas) where the things I was throwing out would go. I designated three categories:

- Storage
- Charity
- Garage Sale

I then started on my task. It was a very cathartic process and I made sure I was ruthless. I stuck to the rules that if the object or thing had no purpose, didn't have any significance, had not be used in the last 12 months, annoyed me or didn't support who I was, it was consigned to one of the three boxes in the garage.

I stuck to my schedule and by the time each room was finished I had a garage full of stuff. I asked one of the local charities to pick up the Charity boxes. I went through the Storage boxes again and realised that most of the stuff wasn't worth saving so I put it in the Garage Sale area.

As I wandered through my house I realised there were many pieces of furniture that didn't suit the house or didn't suit me anymore. My husband was away at the time so I booked a removalist to come in and move all the furniture out of the house. The only things I didn't get rid of were the beds and the two couches that I really liked. Everything else was in the garage. The next Saturday I held a Garage Sale and made quite a lot of money (in the thousands).

With that money I went out and bought one piece of furniture which, by the way, we still have today. I purchased a television cabinet, because with this newfound freedom I seemed to have more energy and wanted to take on more projects. I knew that watching television was merely wasting my life as I watched someone else live theirs. I now had more energy and more time and I was ready to take on the world!

You're probably wondering what my husband said. Well, he came home and looked around the house; he walked around a bit and said that the place echoed. And then, about 24 hours later, he gave me a big hug and said the whole place felt great. He then asked me not to clutter it up again and I promised I wouldn't. We have purchased some choice pieces of furniture over the years but only ones we love, which suit who we are and how we feel. We never make purchases for the sake of filling a space.

This amazing declutter was the first of many. I do this process on a regular basis – at least four times a year. But it is no longer a major event. I can usually get around the whole house in a matter of hours. I no longer have three boxes, I now give everything to charity or I sell it at a Cash Converters. I also encourage my children to do this exercise at the end of each school term.

That part of the story is just the beginning. One of the major benefits about decluttering is that it creates a void in your life – an empty space – which allows new things to come to you. And what happened, not only in my life but in the life of my family, was nothing short of stunning. I don't have the space here to tell you what happened to the whole family so I'll just tell you what happened to me.

The first thing that happened was that I finished a project I had been working on for six years. I had started writing a book back in 1992, but kept putting it back in the filing cabinet then taking it out again; it was an endless drudge. But I decided after the declutter that I would get the book out and finish it and publish it myself. I'd had a number of knock-backs from publishing companies and I didn't want any more disappointments. By July of 1998 (I had finished the declutter in December 1997), the first book came off the press. It was nothing short of amazing and for me a bit of a miracle that I had finally finished it.

I cruised along for the rest of the year, selling my book pretty well but it was certainly not a best seller. By chance, in March 1999 I went to a seminar and one of the surprise speakers was the author of the book on Feng Shui which I had read. As she was speaking I realised I'd missed one room in the house. I could hardly wait to get home and get stuck into that room.

The seminar was on the Thursday and on the Friday I started decluttering the kitchen. I was ruthless. If it was scratched, chipped, broken, not used or I had more of that item than I needed, it went into a box in the garage. I finished on the Sunday and then on the Monday

I asked the assistant who was working with me at the time if she would call one of the magazine shows on one of the major networks to see if they wanted to do an article on me for their show. I had tried to get on this show many times since the publication of my book, but I was never successful. On this day, however, the producer said 'Yes'. Within four days the crew was filming at my house, and guess where they filmed the whole segment? That's right – in my kitchen. The six minute production went to air and the next day my book went to the top of the list – it became a best seller.

The whole realisation of 'when you declutter you create a void and something comes into your life' was beginning to fix hard in my reality. Whenever I want something to happen, I declutter and without fail – something happens.

My husband and I took our three children on the most wonderful two-year trip around Australia. From where we were living in Queensland, the half-way point around the country was Steep Point, the most western piece of land on the Australian continent. A couple of days before we arrived at Steep Point I said to my husband that it would be nice to have an influx of funds so we could continue comfortably for the next year.

He asked me what I was going to do about it and I told him that the first thing I was going to do was clean out the bus we were travelling in. I decluttered our motorhome and packed the box of clutter in the storage compartment until it could be disposed of.

Let me describe Steep Point. It is a remote area where you have to drive almost 200km on corrugated roads to see the beauty of the point and the amazing Zuydorp Cliffs. The only thing there that resembles civilisation is a phone booth. Yes, a phone booth. Our mobile phone had not been in range for quite some time, so I decided to pick up my messages at this amazing remote phone booth. One of the messages was from my publisher, who had decided to publish my second book and give me an advance. That advance took us the rest of the way around Australia. It had happened again! Create a void and something comes into your life. By the way, I had proposed this book to them over a year before. Amazing!

Whenever I speak I always tell a few stories about the power of decluttering. I had one lady who emailed me to tell me that she went home after my talk and decluttered her garage. Within the week she had won a new bike. Another lady who won three door prizes at one of my talks declared after the third prize that only the day before she had cleaned out her linen cupboard. I have heard so many similar stories.

> **Decluttering does not only create a void,
> it also frees up energy and allows abundance to flow.**

Once you have decluttered, it is important to use this freed energy to get yourself organised. There should be a place for everything and everything in its place and with less 'stuff' around, this is easy to achieve.

Don't take my word for it.... Give it a go.

Planning Your Road Map To Success

> *You need to know what you want and when you want it before you can plan how to achieve it.*
> Rachael Bermingham

Everyone talks about goals, and let's face it, we all know what we want right? Wrrrrooonnngggg!!!! Surprisingly most people either don't have a goal, don't know what their goals are, or have had a goal forever that they're not even really interested in achieving anymore. Very few people can pinpoint with crystal clarity what they want and when they want it by.

It's not that we don't know how to achieve goals. There are millions you have already achieved without giving it too much thought. What's that you say? Can't think of any? Well what about walking, talking, reading, writing, learning to ride a bike, drive a car, giving birth, becoming a parent, being a friend, a wife, partner, sharing, looking after yourself, getting a job... The list is endless but being an amazing woman – I can bet you're not done yet!!!

Already you've achieved so much. Some things I can guarantee you're still overwhelmed with (for me I am still overjoyed I made it through 18 hours of natural labour and birthed the most beautiful little spirit into the world!).

You've proven you can set goals AND you've proven you can achieve goals. So why is it so hard for people to achieve more of them?

In my experience, it can be for numerous reasons. Maybe the goal you set was something that you saw in passing and thought that would be nice to have/do' but your heart really wasn't that into it. *Or* it may have been that you set the goal and promptly forgot it. Or *maybe* you set the goal and then didn't know how to go about achieving it? Or could it be that you set the goal and life got in the way? What about, you set the goal and it wasn't clear or detailed enough? Or was it sooooo big that you just thought it was way unachievable?

Whatever the reason, the problem still stands – how do we set *and* achieve our goals?

Here are some steps I use that just may be helpful..... If they have been effective for me, then I'm certain they'll be able to help you too.

First things first: how do we set goals? For most people, this process is a bit hit-and-miss, so here are the steps all laid out for you so you don't have to spend time finding out *how* – instead you can spend your time *acting on them*.

LIPS Tips for Setting Goals

🌿 Take an hour out of your day/week/life to sit down quietly and give some real thought to **what you do really want.** What *do* you want? *Why* do you want it?

🌿 **Make your goals clear,** specific and detailed. Make sure you have a crystal clear view of what your goal is. How does it look, feel, taste, and smell? See yourself having achieved it. How does it feel to have it?

Planning Your Road Map To Success

🖉 **Put a timeline on it.** When do you wish to achieve it by? For example, we wanted to have this book written by 25 December 2005. Be precise.

🖉 **Think big.** The only limitation you have is YOU, so dream big!

🖉 **Keep yourself on track and focused.** If you feel like you can't do it solo, then create a focus group of like-minded people or others also interested in achieving a goal, and keep each other accountable and inspired to succeed.

🖉 **Create a Power Prompt** (affirmation/prayer/intention) that gets you moving. Mine is – I Dream, I Believe, I Create, I Succeed!

🖉 **Write down one new habit per week/month that you will develop to help you achieve what you wish to achieve.** If you wish to get fit, then a good habit would be to get up half an hour earlier and go for a walk; or if you wish to learn something new, then turn the TV off for an hour each night and read or listen to an audio on your chosen topic to assist you in achieving your goals. Again, put a timeline to it and schedule time in your diary so you can remain focused on what you need to do.

🖉 **Write your goals as if you've already achieved them.** I am happy, excited and grateful that I have a beautiful, healthy, happy child! I am so happy that I have positive, passionate, healthy, supportive, prosperous, fun-loving friends in my life.

🖉 **Keep a journal with all the goals you have achieved.** This is fantastic, for when you need to remember that you CAN achieve amazing things – just look at your history and you will be surprised. Remember also to celebrate each achievement when it happens AND to look back on each in the journal and smile!

Now that you've done the ground work it's time to 'do the do' that's doing what it takes to achieve your desires. Here are some tips for you to achieve your dreams.

LIPS Tips for Getting your Goals

Get on with it! I know it's blunt, but you have to stop self-sabotaging by 'creating' reasons why you can't do this, or you didn't have time for that. NOW is the time. Don't waste a minute! Focus *only* on *how* you can achieve your goals.

Implement. This is the number one dream slayer; simple lack of implementation. If you find yourself baulking or procrastinating on doing something, then ask a friend or buddy to help you keep on track. You MUST put in the time and effort!

Surround yourself with supportive, inspiring, positive achievers. Steer clear of anyone negative and remember, don't share your goals with anyone who is likely to run you down about them. Negativity spreads like a disease; don't waste your time and energy there. It isn't constructive. It will not help you achieve your dreams. And if you're in a team – ensure you don't let anyone slow you down in a whole lot of their rigmarole, baggage or fears. Forge ahead, with conviction, determination and a solid strategic plan.

Speak your Power Prompt aloud and proud and with PASSION – every day, twice a day, as often as you can until it's a habit. Repeat it until it has become an automatic thought.

Get a coach or mentor. I've often had coaches and mentors to cheer me on in achieving my goals. Mostly coaches/mentors charge a fee for their services, but there are plenty of coaching schools out there with heaps of new students who need the practice. Some come VERY cheap (if not free), so approach the schools and enquire about being coached by a student. Mentors are different; they've been there done that. They mentor you with what they've already experienced or learnt.

🌿 **Track your progress.** Make sure you can measure or gauge how you are going along the way. Set up a goal-health checklist and each day/week or month visit it to see how you're going.

🌿 **Make choices and decisions with the end in mind.** This will help you make decisions *from* your goals which keep steering you to that end prize.

🌿 **Plan the steps** you need to take and schedule them into your day – just as you 'plan' to do the washing and get it done, so too can you plan to do other less tedious activities that are instrumental in you achieving your goals.

🌿 **Celebrate the little AND big successes and achievements** (read more on this in my achieving success chapter)

🌿 **Have stamina** – anything worth having is worth putting in the time and effort to achieve.

🌿 **Prioritise your goals.** Start with some smaller ones that are achievable so you can get used to the 'feeling of achieving', and celebrate each one. Get excited about them *and* be proud of what you have done to achieve them!

🌿 **Baby Steps.** We all need to start somewhere, but often we wander aimlessly and lose direction on our journey to our goals, so once you know with great clarity what you wish to achieve – you're seeing it, feeling it and getting excited about it – then you need to put a strategy in place, with baby steps that can be checked off as they're accomplished, in order to achieve it. Completing these smaller steps provides momentum and helps to keep you on track.

🌿 **Think about what you need to do or have to succeed.** This is effective for helping you make choices and decisions that will directly or indirectly be helpful in your goal success. If your goal is to save enough money for a house deposit, then going out and making an extravagant purchase (like a car) will directly jeopardise your goal.

🌿 **Be focused, diligent and persistent.** There will be times when you are tired or your confidence takes a little dive, and the quickest way to come out of these emotional lulls is to pull out your journal, speak your Power Prompt and hold your focus with persistence and loyalty to your dreams.

🌿 **Educate yourself** by sourcing, learning and implementing the knowledge you need to move forward.

🌿 **Visualise that you already have it.** Put yourself in the emotion of being the person you wish to be and living the life you desire to be living, having the things you've yearned for.

🌿 **Keep up!** Whenever you think or say something that is negative or energy-sabotaging to your dreams, change the thought immediately to something that is positive and helpful in manifesting your dreams.

🌿 **Think, speak and act well.** The thing that you focus most on often manifests. I often tell the story of how I used to say 'Oh give me a break!' That was until I DID break a bone and now I ensure I am diligent and conscious of always thinking healthy, positive thoughts and focus on what I DO want, not on what I don't want.

🌿 **Share your goals with people who will strive to help you not sabotage you.** Don't waste precious time talking about your goals to people who you KNOW won't be instrumental or positive in your quest.

🌿 **Be thankful.** The more you say thanks and are grateful for what you achieve and receive, the more the Universe/Love/God/Spirit will give you.

Remember you've done this already THOUSANDS of times! Each goal is different in your mind only – no greater, no smaller, it's just a goal -no matter what the size or look of it.

So get out there, and go get them gorgeous!!!!

How to achieve your HEALTH goals

The Real Truth About Food

> *My 7 year old daughter Casie said to me: 'Mummy I figured your book out; God makes all the healthy stuff and everything else is junk'*
> Cyndi O'Meara

Low fat, low calorie, high protein, high fibre, blood type, Pritikin, Atkins, Glycemic Index, Beach – and the list goes on. They all have one thing in common: they are diets, and just some of the many, many diets out there. Each one claims to be the one! When you look at them, each one tells you what type of food to eat and how much.

All diets in the last 50 years have failed for the most part, and if you think that is a harsh judgement, just look at the statistics. Obesity is an epidemic of epic proportions, so if diets are about losing weight then I'd say they have failed. Instead of losing weight the population is gaining it at a far greater rate than is healthy.

My favourite saying applies again: Insanity is doing the same thing and expecting a different result. If you want things to change for you and your family, if you want a different result, then you have to do something that the majority of the population is not doing. Let's look at a few key factors.

Losing Weight vs Gaining Health

First of all, most diets in the marketplace are about losing weight and you know if you lose something you usually find it again. Statistics show that most people who lose weight on a diet are heavier 12 months later than they were when they started. The first three letters in the word diet are 'die' and that's what you feel like when you go on a diet. Dieting is about deprivation and not having fun, because when you go out nothing on the menu suits your diet, or you're not allowed to drink and everything is so tempting, so you just stay home out of harm's way.

Let's see what happens if you change the goal from losing weight to gaining (now I know that's a scary word, but stick with me on this one) – gaining health. All of a sudden you've changed the goal posts. It is no longer a diet of deprivation but rather one where you can eat, but you can only eat foods that make you healthy. You see, low fat, low sugar and low cal are not about health; they are supposedly about weight loss, but the reality is, if you are unhealthy, weight loss is not easy; whereas if you are healthy, weight loss is a side effect, a consequence.

So, Number One New Truth is: Change your goal from losing weight to gaining health. On a lifestyle eating program of gaining health you can have your cake and eat it too.

Quality vs Quantity

Just about every diet on the market now and in the last 50 years has been about what food to eat and how much of it you can eat, counting either calories, fat, sugar, protein or carbohydrates. How novel would it be to not have to worry about *how much you eat* but only about *the quality of the food you eat*? For instance, 'oils ain't oils' and 'milk ain't milk' and 'bread ain't bread'!

When your body is given the right fuel it will have all the energy you need. It will be healthy and able to fight disease and it will set itself at the perfect weight for life. How good does that sound? And it's not hard – it is only a matter of learning a New Truth about food.

Right away we have changed the parameters of eating; no more weight loss diets, no more low-cal, low-fat, high-protein portions; it's now about eating again – eating good food.

But what *is* good? Every day in the papers and on the news and in advertising we're told something new which contradicts what we were told just a year ago. I'm not surprised if most people throw up their hands in horror and just eat what they want. What is the truth? What is good for us? Is it margarine or butter, protein or carbohydrates, sugar or aspartame? People are confused; confused by the advertising, confused by the science, confused by the so called experts.

I'd like to give you a New Truth – *a New Truth about Food* that will fire you up, get you excited, and make you want to change your behaviour around food. This New Truth is so simple you'll say that it's really just common sense, but you need to know that 'common sense' is not so common any more. This New Truth is one of those 'Aha' moments, where you knew you knew it, you just needed it clarified.

I wrote my book Changing Habits Changing Lives over a six-year period and after I finished it my then seven-year-old daughter Casie said to me: "Mummy I figured your book out; God makes all the healthy stuff and everything else is junk'. That awe-inspiring comment was made back in 1999 and it took me a few more years to create a system for showing people how it works.

The system is to divide food into just two groups. The first food group is food from nature; the second food group is food from technology. The chart following is a good example.

The food in the Nature column has mostly been condemned by the so-called experts; the food in the Technology column is the food that has replaced it. The food in the Technology column is the food that is found in almost everything on the supermarket shelves, whereas the food in the nature column is either illegal to buy or hard to find. Yet the foods in the nature column are foods we have survived on and evolved with, living fairly healthy lives, for thousands of years.

The Real Truth About Food

If you look back just 50 years you'll see the dramatic change in our diet, even though on the surface it looks the same. Chocolate cake from the grocery store is not like the chocolate cake made 50 years ago, and the ingredients in the Apple Danish and bread from the bakery today are very different from those used 50 years ago.

Nature-based Foods	Technology-based Food
Raw Milk	Modified Milk
Sea Salt	White Refined Salt
Butter	Margarine
Organic Rolled Oats	Breakfast Cereals
Sugar (Rapadura, Sucanat)	Aspartame and Saccharin
Organic Free-Range Eggs	Eggs or Egg Substitutes
Cold Pressed Oils	Vegetable Oil Hydrogenated or Partially Hydrogenated
Traditional Preserves and Flavourings	Laboratory Additives, Preservatives, Flavourings
Traditional Food Sources	Soy Food

Let's take a look at some of the foods in the table.

Sugar is my all time favourite, as it has been given a bad rap of late. Compared to the alternatives, all those one-calorie, artificial sugars made in a chemical laboratory, sugar is not that bad. But why eat white refined sugar when there are better sugars out there that you may not even know about? White sugar, before it goes to the refinery, goes through a number of processes adding lye, canola oil and icing sugar; bet you didn't know that. By the time it finishes this first lot of processing it is 'raw' sugar; then it goes to another refinery and becomes pure white sugar, with not a drop of nutrition anywhere to be found. Why bother eating that when you can buy sugar that goes through only two processes. Once the sugar cane is cut and crushed, the juice is dehydrated and granulated – nothing added, nothing taken out. Not only do we have sucrose (sugar) but we also have the many nutrients that sugar beets provide when not refined. This sugar can be used in everything from your drinks to baking.

What about **milk?** For thousands of years we have drunk milk pretty much as it came from the cow, then it all went mad. Pasteurisation of milk began back in the late 1950s (this process kills the vital enzyme that helps us digest milk), then 20 years on, homogenisation happened (and we absorb more fat from homogenised milk!) And why do they homogenise milk? So you don't have to shake it! But there is something more sinister about homogenised milk and that is, the fat particles slip straight into the blood stream instead of doing what they should do and go to the lymphatic system first to get cleaned out and then move on to the blood stream. When you play with nature, the consequences can be dire. We keep learning this lesson through food, environment, and many more aspects of our life but for some reason the lesson isn't being learned and we continue to play with nature and cop the consequences.

Salt is another good example. Salt straight from the sea has up to 60 minerals in it, but the salt in the grocery store only has two minerals, and that's because the refineries put it through some gruelling processes including extreme heat. Then, so that it doesn't absorb water, they add chemicals to it. Why not just buy sea salt?

Breakfast cereals are not my favourite food. They start out as nature but with all the processing they end up being very dead, non-nutritious food. In fact, because they are devoid of any nutrition, the manufacturers add a few token vitamins and minerals. Your body needs at least 60 minerals every day for health and thousands of vitamins, glyconutrients and phytonutrients. Breakfast cereals are dead food and if you eat dead food in the morning then you are going to feel dead all day. Try eating live foods in the morning and reap the benefits of vibrant health and energy.

To sum up, it is important to eat the food nature provides, not 'food' that is chemically changed or manipulated by technology, and when you do this you will feel the difference. I believe that if you are going to change your diet you need to do it step by step, by firstly taking a look at your breakfast. Find foods that are alive – Bircher muesli, porridge, eggs, nuts, fruits, and smoothies – to start your day. Once eating an alive breakfast is a habit, then move on to another step. Change from margarine back to butter. Then look at the salt you're eating, and the sugar you use, then onto the milk you drink and cook with. Step by step, bit by bit, it is possible to change your eating and your life.

One of my favourite questions is: If I change my thoughts will my choices change, and if I change my choices will my life change? You bet!!!

In the context of this chapter I'm unable to describe fully what has happened to the foods we eat and what are the best steps to take in order to change your diet for life. For further information go to my website www.changinghabits.com.au and sign up for my monthly educational (sometimes challenging) newsletter!

Healthy Body Healthy Mind

> **Insanity is doing the same thing and expecting a different result**
> Cyndi O'Meara

In my opinion, if you don't have health you don't have energy and if you don't have energy, how do you expect to be a multi-tasking, successful wife, mother, and business woman without burning out?

Good health is not very common in western society; this is easily demonstrated by the statistics with regard to disease. At any one time 40% of a population will have a cold, sniffle or flu; two thirds will contract a terminal illness; one in three will get asthma; one in two will use an illicit drug and one in four will drink alcohol; chronic fatigue is an epidemic and obesity has grown exponentially. Our biggest killers are heart disease, cancer and diabetes – in fact, diabetes has increased 300% in the last 20 years. Do I need to go on? It is obvious that what we are doing in the health care industry is not working. Insanity is doing the same thing and expecting a different result and if you think this situation is going to change, it isn't. In fact the way the health system is now, it will not be able to support itself financially and so something will have to be done.

As I see it, change has to happen on an individual level. People have to start taking responsibility for their own health by taking control of their lifestyles. Founder of the Global Medical Forum, Dr

Ray Levy, says: "A percentage of the population consumes the vast majority of the health-care budget for diseases that are very well known and by large, behavioural; that is – **they're sick because of how they choose to live their lives** and not because of environmental or genetic factors beyond their control."

Take control of your life-style and you can take back control of your life. Now that's easy to say but it is hard to do. I know this because statistics tell us that only one in ten people will change their lifestyle if they are told they have a life-threatening disease and the only way to survive is by changing.

What I find even more alarming is that when I am speaking at a conference and I ask delegates this same question – everyone puts up their hand (agreeing they would make the change) but the reality is, only one in ten will change.

So what makes people change? John Kotter, Harvard University Professor and author of the book *Heart of Change*, says that in order for a company, community or individual to make permanent change, they must first learn a new truth, and then get emotional and excited about the new truth and *then* a change in behaviour will occur.

My purpose is to teach New Truths; not pseudo truths that are in the papers, news, advertisements or on television, but truths that get you fired up so that you want to make changes in order to live a long, happy, healthy, productive life.

Reality is the way we see the world and everyone has a different slant on reality. In order to change, sometimes it is necessary to see the world differently; to find a new paradigm – a New Truth. While most people see the world one way, I mostly see it in a different light, and this is due to my upbringing.

I'm from a very unusual family. My grandfather was a corn farmer in Iowa USA. When the chemical revolution started in the mid 1940s he chose not to use artificial fertilizers or pesticides on his farm. Instead, he continued to farm the old-fashioned way which, in hindsight, was a very smart thing to do. We now have many farmers turning back to the old way of farming; they are called organic and biodynamic farmers. My father, who lived in New Zealand, was a pharmacist and after several years of pharmacy he decided that what he was doing was not helping people but hurting them and making them sicker. In particular, he noticed one client in her seventies who came in over a year and was sprightly and healthy in the beginning but by the year's end she had turned into a very sick lady. What had happened to her happened to many of his customers. They started with one prescription and then six or so weeks later were in for another prescription that merely counteracted the side-effect of the first, until, by the end of the year, these customers were on many medications. The medications were not helping the problem but rather, over time, were exacerbating the sickness. So he left pharmacy in the mid 1950s and flew to Iowa to become a chiropractor. My Dad was one of the first chiropractors in Australia in the early 1960s.

While my father was in Iowa he met my mother who was a nurse and with their new truth about health and wellbeing they made a decision that they would not give any of their children any form of medication unless it was a life threatening situation. I'm 48 this year and I've never taken any form of medication. This is not luck; this is good life style and health management!

Just to add further to this, my mother was the eldest of 11 children, seven of whom were boys, and six of these boys were haemophiliacs who contracted AIDS in the early 1980s from contaminated blood. Two wives and a child of one of the brothers also contracted AIDS. Over a period of several years, all but one died; eight deaths in all, from one family. It is interesting to note here that each one of my mother's brothers was given the drug of choice at that time, AZT, which, in my opinion, killed them faster than the disease would have. There was only one brother who chose not to go the medical route but rather chose diet, exercise, positive mental attitude, supplementation and overall healthy living. He managed to live many, many more years and finally died while taking part in an experimental drug trial. That might sound harsh but he was asked to participate in a drug trial. The trial consisted of two groups. The first group took the drug they were testing and the second group took a placebo. The participants did not know what they were taking. My bet was that my uncle was taking the experimental drug.

With my parents' values and the tragedy of my mother's brothers, I have learnt a very healthy disrespect for drugs and medications – although they do have their place but that place is not for everyday health issues. I have brought my own children up the way my parents taught me, with healthy living, good food, active lifestyle and no medications. My children are 19, 17 and 14 and their systems are clean – they have not had any medications. And it's not as if we have not had childhood illnesses or broken bones; they have been a part of our life. But, just as my parents taught me, I have taught my children that pain relief, enhanced immunity and the fighting of disease comes from a source within, not an external source. If we don't let the body fight the baby fights without resorting to outside help, how is the body ever going to be able to fight the big fights as we get older? More and more people's immune systems are compromised by not allowing the body to do the work.

Looking internally for help means that help is always to hand. This is so needed in this day and age where our young people and older people look for an external crutch for their everyday problems, and not only health problems. When we are so willing to give antiinflammatories or pain killers on a daily basis to ourselves and our children, then as our children grow up they learn that it is an external force that makes them feel better. So, when they are offered an illicit drug such as marijuana, cocaine or ecstasy and told that it will make them feel better, they have no qualms about taking it because that is the way they have always been taught to feel better – to *take* something.

This is a truth that we need to know. We have become complacent, believing the little white pill will make us better when in fact it doesn't do that; it merely takes away the signal that something is wrong. A pain in the knee tells you that something is wrong; if you take a pain killer or anti-inflammatory, that is exactly the same as cutting the wire to the red light in your car that signals there is something wrong in the motor. The problem doesn't go away – you have merely taken away the signal that tells you something is wrong – and you continue to use your knee and cause harm to it until eventually the pills don't work anymore and the knee is permanently damaged.

Now I'm not saying that anyone on medications should stop taking them. What I am saying is that complacency is not a good thing. Find a new way to health by taking on the responsibility of a healthy lifestyle. Don't smoke, don't drink or eat excessively, do exercise, take time out of your busy life, do things that you love, take holidays, eat healthy food, and live by the 80/20 rule where 80% of the food you eat is healthy and 20% is enjoying the foods you love which may not necessarily be healthy. When you begin to make healthy lifestyle choices, your body immediately begins to get healthy and the need for medications is reduced and the time taken for being sick and tired diminishes.

When taking on the challenge of a healthy lifestyle and changing your diet and exercise, I suggest you consult a professional before going off any medications.

Moods, Food and the Mind

> *The quality of your food affects the quality of your thinking which affects the quality of your mood which affects the quality of your life.*
> Cyndi O'Meara

Just think about this: over the past 30 years, and particularly in the past five years, the rate of depression and anxiety has increased enormously. In the western world alone, depression is one of the most debilitating and expensive illnesses, costing billions of dollars a year. One in five westerners has some form of mental illness and around 6 per cent suffer serious depression. Considering most people are materially better off today and enjoy more convenience than existed just 30 years ago, you have to wonder what has caused the increase. Is it the pressures of the world, or is it a result of the foods we eat affecting the brain chemicals that balance mood, which in turn affects our coping skills?

There are three main chemical neurotransmitters in the brain that help send messages from one cell to the next. They are dopamine, noradrenaline and serotonin. Dopamine and noradrenalin are the brain chemicals that keep us alert; they have a tendency to make us think more quickly and they increase motivation, mental acuity and productivity. Serotonin, on the other hand, is the calming brain chemical – it produces a relaxed, more focused, less anxious, less stressed, more euphoric feeling. *Our levels of these neurotransmitters are directly related to the foods we eat.*

Now I can see you reading with anticipation to find out which foods increase or decrease these chemicals, as there are always times in our life when we wish to have one or the other mood. It's quite simple really: proteins – such as meat, fish, eggs, freshly shelled nuts, yoghurt, cheese, legumes and complementary proteins – cause an increase in the brain chemicals for alertness (dopamine and noradrenaline), while carbohydrates – such as wheat, rye, millet, oats, rice, bread, pasta and starchy vegetables – cause an increase in the brain-calming chemical, serotonin.

The brain synthesises these chemicals (neurotransmitters) from the amino acids tryptophan and tyrosine. (Amino acids, which are the building blocks of protein, are also present as individual amino acids in carbohydrates.) As tyrosine is the precursor to dopamine and noradrenaline, and tryptophan creates serotonin, you would think that an indulgence of protein with these two key precursors would cause all three chemical neurotransmitters to increase in the brain, thus causing calmness with alertness at the same time. But not so – once again the ingenuity of the body is such that this doesn't happen.

The more protein you eat, the greater the tyrosine levels in your blood, thus causing an increase in the alertness chemicals in the brain (dopamine and noradrenaline). But this is not true for tryptophan. Tryptophan, tyrosine and four other amino acids enter the brain through the blood brain barrier (BBB), competitively, via the same mechanism. When we eat a protein, tyrosine and the four other amino acids become plentiful while tryptophan becomes scarce, therefore very little tryptophan can pass through the BBB. But when we eat a meal of carbohydrates, tyrosine and the other four amino acids become scarce, while tryptophan found in carbohydrates becomes the dominating amino acid, thus passing through the BBB easily with very little competition.

LIPS Tips for Choosing your mood by choosing your food.

Calming Carbohydrates All carbohydrates are not equal in their ability to offer mood-altering results. The best way to consume carbohydrates is in the form of whole grains and complex carbohydrates. Oats, millet, cracked wheat, buckwheat and rice are prime examples. Whole grains are broken down over a long period of time, keeping a constant flow of serotonin in our brain. To experience the maximum effect of carbohydrates on your mood, it is important to eat them without any protein.

Peppy Proteins If you're feeling sluggish, protein power can produce the effect you want. Protein encourages the production of dopamine and noradrenaline which produce alertness, mental energy and quicker reaction time. The effects of eating protein last about two to three hours. To maximise the 'arousal' effect of a protein meal, limit the intake of fat and carbohydrates. If you are not a good sleeper it is important not to eat protein for several hours before bedtime or you may experience difficulty falling asleep.

Neutral Fruit and Vegetables Most fruits and vegetables are mood-neutral foods, so you can consume them without affecting your mood. If you're feeling the way you want to feel, a meal of fruit or a healthy salad might be the best option.

Sabotaging Fatty Foods Fatty foods cause havoc with moods. An overburden of fats means digestion overload, causing a large portion of blood flow to leave the brain and be shunted to the digestive tract to help with digestion and absorption, thus causing a condition I call 'brain fag'. The brain simply stops working at peak efficiency and goes into slow mode, causing tiredness, forgetfulness, lack of concentration and all other mind-confusing, unwanted feelings. (By the way, a very large indulgent meal will also give the same symptoms.)

🌿 **Antagonising Alcohol** Difficulty walking, blurred vision, slurred speech, slow reaction times, impaired memory, aggression, confusion, amorous, super mellow, – clearly, alcohol affects the brain and our moods. Alcoholism destroys the brain, but current research shows that moderate alcohol consumption increases blood flow to the brain, which seems to suggest a link with improved mental function. The results of the research show some specificity in the association between alcohol consumption and cognitive ability. Research at University College, London, has found that those who drink only one glass of wine a week have significantly sharper thought processes than teetotalers.

🌿 **Exhilarating Caffeine** While caffeine is an addictive drug it can also be a very useful tool for changing moods and states of alertness. Scientists have developed various theories to explain caffeine's wake-promoting and mind-altering power. It seems to interfere with the chemical adenosine, which is a natural sleeping pill made by the body. Caffeine has been shown to enhance mood and increase alertness; in moderate amounts it's potent for athletes, students, brain-storming committees and the like. Used wisely, and not as an hourly pick-me-up, caffeine taken as tea or coffee can alter brain performance, making it a very useful tool.

🌿 **Outstanding Omega-3 Fatty Acids** Omega-3 fatty acids, found in oily fish like salmon and mackerel as well as many nuts, like walnuts, can help stave off depression. Recent research has revealed that omega-3 is excellent for improving concentration and energy levels.

🌿 **Helpful Herbs** Herbs have been used for centuries, not only for flavour in cooking but as natural remedies too. Ginger can lift the spirit, cinnamon counteracts exhaustion, camomile helps with nervous tension, while peppermint can be taken to help calm nerves and relieve anger. Basil is thought to clarify the mind, so try a large batch of pesto stirred through some healthy pasta to give your mind clarity.

🌿 **Vital Vitamins and Minerals** B-vitamins play an important role in brain function. B6 helps to convert tryptophan into serotonin, vitamin B1 helps build and maintain healthy brain cells, and folic acid is also an essential brain food. Zinc is a mineral that helps keep the senses sharp as well as encouraging a healthy immune system – it is critical for proper growth and development of the nervous system.

🌿 **Stimulating Sunlight.** The sun inhibits a hormone in the brain called melatonin. This hormone creates a calmness in the brain and gets the body and mind ready for sleep. It is a hormone that is needed at night so it is produced when the sun goes down; but during the day exposure to sunlight will help keep melatonin at bay and enhance the alert state of the brain, as well as help to get rid of the blues.

🌿 **Overboard Overeating** also creates mood changes. For example, what do you want to do straight after Christmas dinner? The usual answer is, have a siesta. What has happened is that your digestive system is overloaded, so some of the blood from the brain, arms and legs is shunted to the digestive system to help in the process of delivering the food's nutrients to the rest of the body. That's why when you eat too much food you either want to sleep or you find it hard to get physically motivated. If you don't digest the food within six hours or so then it begins to putrefy, releasing toxins into the blood and creating havoc with energy and mood.

You can use the principles of Food–Mood Connection in relation to sports performance. While peak performance of the physical body is important for athletes, many times the mind is the edge that makes the difference. Using the foods that cause alertness in the brain can make all the difference between winning and losing.

If you are someone who finds it hard to sleep at night, to help improve your sleep patterns it would be beneficial to have protein for lunch and carbohydrates for dinner. Stop drinking all caffeine drinks at midday, don't eat any protein after lunch and make sure you sleep in a dark room. Just see what a difference it makes when your brain is calmed down.

If you want the upper hand at a business meeting, then eat smart. To keep your brain sharp and alert it is important to be aware of the Food–Mood Connection. Two basic rules are: eat very little fat and eat your protein first. So, a good business lunch would be a clear soup (hold the bread and butter), then fish (without sauce) and a salad and steamed vegetables (hold the alcohol). For dessert, have fruit salad – sorry, no cake or puddings. Watch what your lunch partner eats and see who has the upper hand by the end of the meal.

Sitting down and listening to a speaker, either at a conference, university lecture or school, can sometimes become tiring. Usually, during the morning sessions most people are alert and full of questions, but after lunch the yawns start and heads start to nod. The food that is offered at lunch is often starchy, full of breads, cheeses and other foods that cause drowsiness.

My suggestion is that at morning tea, don't touch the sweet pastries; just have a cup of coffee and some fruit if they are on offer. Then at lunch choose one type of meat and salad, with coffee and fruit again for afternoon tea. Using this strategy should make a difference by keeping you alert all day, allowing the brain to take in the information needed.

If you're a shift worker, to allow yourself to work to the best of your ability it is important to manipulate the foods you eat to match when you want to sleep and when you want to be awake. Make sure that throughout your shift you eat foods to increase alertness, and then, when you are ready to sleep, eat foods that increase the brain-calming chemicals. It is also very important that you sleep in a dark room. The darker the room the more abundant melatonin is, to help you sleep and heal.

With this awareness of the Food–Mood Connection, you can use your food as a powerful tool to enhance performance in all areas of life. Parents can also use these principles to help children manage their busy lives.

From the time you wake up until approximately four hours before bed, try and consume some type of protein. For breakfast, include eggs or fish or consume a complementary protein, which includes porridge or toast with nuts. Avoid refined breakfast cereals and starchy breakfasts like toast and jam. Snacks for morning and afternoon tea should be nuts and yoghurt or a mix of crackers and nut butters or hummus and other protein dips rather than muffins, cakes or cookies. Lunch should also have some protein, like salmon, beef or chicken, with vegetables. Then at night you can have pasta, rice and other high-carbohydrate meals.

Quality of Food Not only do we need to think about the type of food to eat for managing moods, the quality of the food we eat is also very important. The brain is a pharmacy, manufacturing chemicals for every thought and every connection between the brain neurons. If you give the brain pharmacy the right ingredients then it will manufacture top class neurotransmitters and brain chemicals. Give the brain the wrong foods in the way of hydrogenated vegetable oils, intersterification fats, margarine, artificial sweeteners, additives, modified milks, preservatives and the like then the quality of the brain chemicals is severely compromised. Depression has increased along with the increase in technology and manipulated foods we now eat. This correlation is one not to over-look, make sure the quality of the food you eat is from nature and not technology foods in order to make brain chemicals for correct brain function, thinking and moods.

Plan Your Day It intrigues me that the typical western diet is carbohydrates for breakfast and lunch, and then protein for dinner, and that most of the foods eaten on a daily basis are modified by science and technology. If your moods and your sleeping patterns are not working for you, try changing and manipulating the foods you eat in order to change the brain neurotransmitters to those that best suit your needs.

Statisticians and health experts expect depression to be the most debilitating and most costly disease by the year 2020. It doesn't need to be. Our knowledge of the brain and its neurotransmitters clearly shows us that food is an important part of making sure this amazing complexity of chemicals and neurons runs efficiently. If you want quality thinking and you don't want to be a part of this destructive epidemic that affects many members of our society from teenagers to the elderly and every social strata, then re-read the section about which foods affect your mind and moods and choose accordingly. Make sure the quality of your thinking reflects the quality of your food ... which affects the quality of your thinking which affects the quality of your mood which affects ... By changing the quality of your thinking you then change the quality of your life.

The Truth On Beauty

> *'How you present yourself to the world reflects your own sensuality, beauty and spirit. Love the body you are in; groom it, nourish it, exercise it and pamper it, then you will radiate an energy that is truly beautiful'*
> Kim Morrison & Fleur Whelligan

Have you ever thought about what it is that makes some women truly beautiful? How some women radiate a certain energy that is so appealing regardless of their age?

The commonality is, they have a 'presence.' They have a way of walking, talking and being. They know themselves well. They feel confident and are quite content to be in their own skin.

Real beauty isn't about a flawless, wrinkle-free complexion. It is not about looking like the beauty queens we see in the fashion magazines, it's not about designer clothes or the biggest jewels. It is about honouring, respecting and loving yourself. It may sound corny but it is true.

Real beauty is natural beauty. It is nurturing your body and skin with the best possible attention and nourishment you can – inside and out.

Skin care, hair care and makeup play an important role for a lot of women. Let's face it, most of us enjoy looking and feeling our best, we love pampering our bodies and skin and taking a little time out to indulge ourselves.

But in today's world achieving natural beauty can be very confusing. How can you make the best choices when there seem to be a hundred instant solutions being sold to you? 'Wrinkle free in 10 days', 'See the difference overnight', 'The ultimate anti-ageing solution'.

It all seems so unreal. In fact just the words 'anti-ageing' show us how society has got it all wrong. It is inevitable – we are all going to age. But perhaps our intention should be to 'age gracefully' with dignity and poise, for with age also comes wisdom and an understanding that loving yourself unconditionally (wrinkles and all) is the only way to real happiness and fulfillment in life.

The beauty industry is a multi-billion dollar industry. There is so much money being spent in the scientific community on research into skincare, but no matter how clever man is at replicating certain ingredients or constituents of the plant and sea world, Mother Nature still reigns supreme with her healing and rejuvenating properties. So much so that nearly every beauty company is spending thousands, if not millions, trying to capture this in a jar – often without a thought on how to do this the most natural way.

These are exciting times though, as finally it seems people are becoming more aware that what you put on to your skin does in fact matter! A beauty revolution is taking place.

Your skin is a living, breathing organ that can easily absorbs ingredients present in skincare products, many of which can compromise your health and immunity. But rather than just relying on the sales pitch you get from a person selling product to you, it is becoming increasingly important to be an informed customer and know what you are looking for. You don't want to buy into the 'anti-ageing' hype;

you want pure and natural products that support your skin to age gracefully – products that care for your body and our planet holistically, because that is what we all deserve.

Nowadays, as consumers become more savvy and demand more truly natural products, we find we can indeed have it all. There are companies out there now that are willing and able to provide products that are natural and safe; products that support our skin to function and rejuvenate at the highest level, while also supporting our health. And products that work *with* nature, not against it.

Did you know that women expose themselves to over 200 chemicals a day through their daily personal care products? Scary thought isn't it? The following is a list of ingredients found in skincare and personal care products. There are the goodies which flood your skin with nature's nutrition, and then there are the nasties, which you may choose to avoid for your skin and health's sake. From being carcinogenic, DNA-damaging, hormone-disrupting or known irritants, many of these ingredients are under further investigation in various countries and therefore should be avoided. It may be interesting to check your beauty and personal care products and see how many of them contain these ingredients. The ingredients listed here have all come under serious question in the last few years.

The Nasties

Sodium Lauryl Sulphate (SLS): although originating from an alcohol found in coconut oil, there are many chemical processes used in the final product. SLS may damage the outer layers of the skin causing dryness, dermatitis and blocked pores. It may also enhance the absorption of other chemicals. The US National Toxicology Programme (NTP) classifies it as a skin and eye irritant. In fact, when dermatologists want to test the calming effect of an ingredient, they use Sodium Lauryl Sulphate as the irritant! Many soaps, toothpastes, shampoos and baby care products (yes, baby care) contain this ingredient.

Mineral Oil and Petrolatum Products: these are semi-solid hydrocarbons that have been purified to some extent. Insoluble in water, they are used as a barrier on the skin. They give products a nice feel and slip; however they offer no nutritional value and leave a 'plastic' film on the skin which impairs healthy skin function. They are inexpensive and commonly used in skincare.

Isopropyl Alcohol: used as a solvent, this is a denatured alcohol which is highly poisonous if ingested or inhaled in large doses. It is used in cosmetics, hair colours, body lotions and anti-freeze solutions. Its safety for use in skincare is under serious question.

Paraben Preservative: a common preservative used by many skin care companies to allow products excellent shelf life. It is currently being investigated as there is a question around its ability to disrupt healthy hormone function within the body.

Propylene Glycol: used as a moisture-carrying agent and solvent, it is also known as anti-freeze. There have been questions about its safety since the early 1990s. It is used a lot in make-up, deodorants, baby products, lipsticks and suntan lotions. The NTP classify it as a skin and eye irritant.

Diethanolamine (DEA) and Tiethanolamine (TEA): these are emulsifiers and detergents. Studies show they can be irritating to the skin and mucous membranes. Both are under question due to the possible link to cancer in laboratory animals.

Imadazolidinyl Urea: another commonly used preservative which may cause irritation and dermatitis. It may also form formaldehyde in the cells. Used in baby products, skincare and makeup.

Amines: these are organic compounds derived from ammonia. Mainly used in hair dyes, they are under serious investigation by the American Cancer Society.

Artificial Colours: usually listed as 'pigment' or dye' on the label, it should be noted that all artificial colours may be detrimental to your health. A lot of them are found in children's personal care products and in makeup. They are synthetically produced and can cause many skin irritations. Natural Iron Oxides are the safe alternative.

Aluminium: most commonly used in deodorants. Aluminium blocks the sweat-glands, which prevents the body's normal perspiration and elimination processes. There is question as to how much the body absorbs this ingredient, particularly as it is placed directly into the lymph node area under the arm, and it is mixed with other chemicals and preservatives to create the final product.

Polyethylene Glycols (PEGs): these are synthetic polymers, used with many different base ingredients to create binders, emulsifiers and humectants. There are more natural and safer alternatives.

Animal Products: manufacturers avoid writing 'animal' on ingredients lists. Animal products are also known as Collagen Amino Acids, Elastin Amino Acids or Epiderm Oil R. These ingredients are made from the tissue, cartilage, bone and connective tissue of animals: usually cows, pigs and sheep.

The Goodies

It is an exciting time in the health and beauty industry. As awareness grows surrounding the skin and its impact on our health, we are seeing more responsible companies offering us safe and very effective products. These companies are looking very seriously at the science of the skin and combining that with the best quality, natural plant-sourced ingredients. As this industry is constantly evolving we can look forward to the latest cutting-edge information on how to keep our skin at its optimum, while supporting our health and protecting the environment. The following list is an example of some of the wonderful ingredients that come from Mother Nature.

Pure Essential Oils: these special oils are known as the life force of the plant. They are approximately 70 times more concentrated than the plant or herb they came from. Extracted from leaves, roots, resins, flowers, grasses and fruit, they have the ability to penetrate the skin to produce therapeutic effects, and also affect us emotionally and mentally with their powerful aromas. Used in skincare, they not only add therapeutic properties but also help to stabilise and preserve products.

Plant and Nut Oils: these include Rosehip, Jojoba, Carrot, Evening Primrose, Pecan, Olive, Avocado, Calendula, Sweet Almond, Wheatgerm, Hypericum, Sesame, Hazelnut and others. These wonderful oils nourish, soften and supply the skin with essential fatty acids that help with tissue repair and regeneration. Only cold-pressed oils should be used as these retain their high quantities of vitamins, minerals and antioxidants and have undergone fewer processes.

Manuka Honey: this is Nature's sugar. It has skin-softening, moisturising and healing properties and has been used in natural skincare for hundreds of years. Manuka honey has special antiseptic qualities that make it a wonderful support and healer to the skin.

Shea Butter: this is a very nourishing and moisturising product that leaves a protective film on the skin. This wonderful vegetable fat is extracted from the nuts of the Karite tree.

Wheat Straw Extract: this is also known as cetearyl alcohol. Different from normal alcohol which is drying on the skin, cetearyl alcohol contains fatty alcohols which help to emulsify ingredients in a product. This is an effective and safe alternative to the chemical emulsifiers used.

Waxes: Beeswax: is another natural emulsifier, which has great softening and lubricating properties. *Candelilla wax:* adds body and slip to products, and is obtained from the coating of the wax slipper plant. *Carnauba wax*: is used for texture and as a gloss agent, and is obtained by scraping the wax off the Brazilian Wax Palm tree. *Orange Peel wax:* is an emollient with great stabilizing properties.

Herbal Extracts like:

- *Echinacea*: is anti-inflammatory and calming on the skin.

- *Eye Bright Herb*: has antiseptic and anti-inflammatory properties.

- *Pine Bark Extract*: is a good skin protector as it has strong anti-oxidant properties.

- *St. John's Wort*: is very healing with vaso-constricting properties which are great for dilated capillaries.

- *Burdock Root*: indicated for healing inflammatory skin conditions.

- *Wild Pansy*: has known UVA and UVB screening properties, so assists with sun protection; it also functions as an anti-oxidant and preservative.

- *Yarrow*: is mildly disinfecting with great soothing properties for irritated skin.

- *Horsetail herb*: which has a high content of the mineral Silica, which builds healthy skin, hair and nails.

Gels:

- *Harakeke*: a plant in plentiful supply in New Zealand which provides a wonderful gel with healing and soothing properties.

- *Aloe Vera*: is more commonly known, however this gel is extremely hard to stabilize in a product once extracted. The best way to get the wonderful healing benefits from this plant is to grow your own and pick a stem off as you need it; great for spots and wound healing.

🌿 Clays have been used for centuries to clean, purify and revive the skin. There are many different types of clays - indicated for different skin types, but all have the ability to remove dead skin cells and stimulate the lymph and blood to the area, resulting in fresher, clearer skin.

The products you choose to use on your face, hair and body are vitally important. Become more aware of what you are actually applying to your precious skin, look at the questionable ingredients, check out various websites to research their effects for yourself and if in doubt ask the manufacturers. Just be aware that for every question raised about an ingredient, a manufacturer will have a scientific answer as to why it is perfectly ok to be included. And even though an ingredient may be classified as toxic, for example, regulations and legislation may have approved a certain level included in certain products as in fact 'safe'. This chapter has been written so you become more aware of the many questionable ingredients large companies are presently using, but also to let you know there are some marvellous companies out there who carry a wonderful ethos that supports and cares for our health, our environment and our beautiful planet and are committed to being truly safe and natural.

Your Daily Skin Care Ritual

Each one of us is unique, and this individuality is mirrored in our skin. Learning to understand and recognise your skin's needs is an important step to achieving a healthy complexion. Whether you have an oily, normal, dry, combination or sensitive skin, it will react to what is happening in your life; stress, poor nutrition, lack of exercise, hormonal changes, environment changes and lack of sleep all will have an effect.

There are some basic skincare rules that apply to everyone:

🌿 **Your skin needs to be gently cleansed.** Now *gentle* is the key word here as this is the step that most people overdo. In cleansing the skin we are removing makeup and sweat and oils, while leaving the skin fresh and relaxed to receive nourishment. If we overcleanse the skin as some foaming cleansers and soaps do, we are often left with the squeaky-clean feeling. This squeaky clean feeling indicates we have stripped all the moisture from the top layers of the skin. In other words, we have dehydrated it. This over-cleansing also stimulates the skin to try and produce more oil to compensate, and therefore creates a skin imbalance. A gentle, milky cleanser that is removed with water and a warm flannel is usually the best choice for most skin types. For an oily skin a mild cleansing gel may be used in combination with your milky cleanser.

NB: The eye area consists of very delicate tissue. To remove eye makeup use a special eye makeup remover consisting of nourishing oils. Calendula oil is one of the best.

Your skin needs toning and hydrating. This step can be a little confusing for some. Toning is not to remove the last traces of cleanser. The cleansing process should be complete on its own, otherwise your cleanser has not done its job. Toning is to freshen, hydrate and prepare the skin for nourishment. This can be in the form of a hydrating aromatic water, or a gel which draws moisture to the skin. Avoid toners that contain alcohol, as these will only dehydrate the skin.

Your skin needs moisture and nourishment. The average life of a skin cell is about 28 days, therefore a spectrum of different nutrients is needed to create and nurture these new cells. This is both an inside and an outside job. Good nutrition (see Cyndi's chapter) will produce healthy skin cells going to the surface of your skin, while good nourishment from the outside will ensure they get the support they need. A good moisturizer will deliver both hydration (moisture) and nourishment. Your skin needs essential fatty acids, antioxidants and vitamin and mineral support, as well as healing ingredients, to give it strength and protection from the environment.

NB: Extra nourishment can be delivered at night time with specific night products, as your skin regenerates and repairs itself while you sleep.

Your Weekly Skin Care Rituals

Add a couple of weekly treatments to your daily rituals and you will soon see your skin flourish even more:

Exfoliation: This is an important step as it helps remove all the dead skin cells that are consistently being brought to the surface; removing them helps all your nourishing products to work more effectively. They come in the form of clay-based peels, gentle soft scrubs and exfoliating masks. Avoid gritty scrubs as these scratch the surface of the skin and can over stimulate.

Masks: For an oily skin a deep cleansing clay mask once or twice weekly will remove excess oil and prevent blockages and breakouts. For a normal to dry skin, a rich hydrating plant mask once a week will add extra hydration and nutrition to the skin to give it back its glow.

Hair Care

Like the skin, your hair reflects inner health and wellbeing. There is no doubt that if you are eating well, exercising and getting adequate sleep chances are your hair will show this. However many people find that having a 'bad hair day' can actually be a regular occurrence. Your hair type is largely, genetically predetermined and if you have fine limp hair or are suffering hair loss prematurely then you can look to your parents (and sometimes grandparents) to see where it came from.

Some believe that a head of beautiful hair can only be achieved by using extravagantly advertised products that promise to miraculously change dry, dull and brittle hair to shiny, healthy and strong hair within days of using the product. Commercial shampoos are not magic potions; they are a chemical blend of waxes, detergents and other ingredients to make our hair appear shiny and healthy. Basically they are made with the same formula as carpet shampoos. One of the main ingredients is Sodium Lauryl Sulphate (SLS, one of the nasties), an emulsifying agent also found in engine degreasers. Charming! For most, lathering is a good sign of cleansing, but a lot of the time that is purely for our satisfaction – so they appear to be working.

If you really like your shampoo, regardless of the ingredients, then at least try diluting it by half with water. Detergent-based shampoos may actually strip the hair of its natural oils, which is often the reason a conditioner is required.

All the time and money spent to gain a head of fantastic hair is going to be largely wasted if nutrition is inadequate, there is undue stress or a lack of sleep. Get back to basics. Look at all aspects of your health and, again, check the ingredients of your hair care products. There are some fantastic, more natural hair care products on the market. It may take you a while to find one you like but it will be worth it once you do. Remember, if you do change your hair care products to more natural ones then allow at least 21-28 days before you make a judgement about them as it may take a few weeks for your hair to adjust to the less harsh ingredients.

LIPS Tips for taking care of your hair:

🌿 Choose the most natural shampoo and conditioner that you can at a health food store, or a hairdresser specialising in natural or organic products..

🌿 Wash your hair 2 times per week (more often if it gets really dirty!) Too much washing makes dry hair drier and oily hair even more oily.

🌿 Buy the best hairbrush you can afford. Pure bristles are the best. Make sure they are rounded, not rough or sharp. Wash your hairbrush regularly – once a week – and use essential oils like Tea Tree to help keep it clean.

🌿 Do not put your hair up too tightly. It may cause headaches and literally pull your hair out.

🌿 Chemicals and heat can dry out your hair and make it brittle. If you don't do either of these things but still have brittle hair, then look to your diet. Increase the essential fatty acids in your diet by eating more deep sea fish, or salmon, or take a dessertspoon of flaxseed oil in a smoothie or in vegetable and salad dressings daily.

🌿 Rinse or, better still, wash your hair as soon after swimming as possible. Chlorinated and salt water can be damaging to your hair. Be careful if you swim often though, a swimming cap may be advisable.

🌿 Use a wide-toothed comb or your fingers to arrange wet hair. Wet hair is very elastic and can be badly damaged by harsh brushing, fine toothed combs or rough handling.

🌿 Regular scalp massage can increase blood flow to the scalp, stimulate the hair follicles and improve the condition of your hair. There is nothing nicer and more relaxing than having someone do this for you and often this is the perfect treat at the hairdressers!

🌿 Do a Warm Oil Treatment on your hair at least once a month. Put 20mls of a cold pressed base oil like jojoba or sweet almond into the top of a ceramic vaporiser. Add 10 drops total of your chosen essential oils. Light the candle to warm the oil and blow out once desired temperature is reached. Do not allow oil to get too hot. Place a towel around your shoulders. Now part your dry hair with a comb and paint the oil blend onto the scalp and roots using a natural bristle pastry brush. Comb through with a wide-toothed comb and leave in for a minimum of one hour. Better still, wrap your hair in cling film and leave in overnight for optimum results. Because oil is not soluble in water, apply shampoo to the oiled hair before wetting it. Wash and condition as usual and rinse with an aromatic hair rinse (see below).

Essential Oils to Use for Warm Oil Treatment:

(Choose three oils – 10 drops total – for each condition)
- *Alopecia   Clary Sage, Lavender, Rosemary, Thyme
- *Dry Hair   Sandalwood, Rosewood, Ylang Ylang, Cedarwood, Geranium, Lavender
- *Oily Hair   Cypress, Cedarwood, Clary Sage, Lemon, Lavender *Normal Hair Rosemary, Lemon, Cedarwood, Lavender
- *Flaky Scalp   Lavender, Patchouli, Rosewood.
- *Dandruff   Tea Tree, Cedarwood, Lemon, Eucalyptus, Sandalwood .
- *Split Ends   Rosewood, Palmarosa, Sandalwood, Geranium .

Aromatic Hair Rinses are a great way to add shine and lustre to your hair. They help nourish the scalp and, by leaving a small residue of oil on the hair, can help protect it and create an aromatic aroma. Simply fill a 100ml glass blending bottle with warm water, add 4 drops of your chosen essential oils and shake. Wash and condition your hair as usual, turn off the shower and squeeze excess water from your hair. Shake the blending bottle containing essential oils and water and sprinkle contents all over your head, hair and body. Massage the aromatic rinse into your scalp and towel dry your hair. Style as usual.

- *Dark Hair   1 drop Geranium, 1 drop Lavender, 2 drops Rosewood
- *Light Hair   2 drops Rosemary, 1 drop Chamomile, 1 drop Lemon
- *Red Hair   1 drop Orange, 2 drops Geranium, 1 drop rankincense

The Home Spa

There are times when we all need to take refuge from the demands of our busy lives. Being able to retreat from the world to soothe, relax and re-energize over-tired bodies is often all it takes to rebalance and recharge. The ultimate treat would be to book into a resort or spa and indulge in the many treatments available. However, finding the time or money to do so can often be a problem. That is where creating your own home spa can be the ultimate alternative.

Many spa programmes help you to detox, relax, restore, balance, strengthen and heal. Things like sweat. Your nose may start to run as well! Steaming is very cleansing and refreshing. You can make your own masks by using things like fresh herbs cut finely, oatmeal, water, Fullers earth clay, egg white and lemon juice. Use natural masks to ensure you limit or avoid synthetic or harmful ingredients. It is wise not to overcleanse the skin; having a facial mask once a week is more than adequate.

Eye and Face Refreshers Placing soaked chamomile tea bags on the eyes when you're feeling fatigued or have a tension headache can do wonders. Making a spritzer by filling a 100ml bottle with water and adding 6 drops total of your essential oils and using as a facial spray is very refreshing and helps to hydrate and tone the skin. Favourite essential oils for the face are: Rose, Lavender, Eucalyptus, Lime, Palmarosa, Rosewood and Geranium.

Self Massage Every morning before you get dressed try the full body aromatic body rub. Simply place approximately 6mls (just over a teaspoon) of cold pressed base oil like sweet almond into a small glass bowl. Add 3 drops total of your chosen essential oils, depending on how you feel. Mix and then rub briskly over the whole body from toes to head. Use only a small amount of oil so that your clothes do not absorb the oils; your skin is supposed to do this and you want to feel glowing not greasy!

Hair Rinse Fill a 100ml blending bottle with warm water and add 4-6 drops of your chosen essential oils. Wash and condition hair as normal then, before you hop out of the shower, shake the bottle and pour it all over your head. Dry and style your hair as you usually do.

🍃 **Body Brushing** Taking a natural bristle body brush into the shower or bath is a fantastic way to revitalise tired skin. Add a few drops of your favourite essential oil to the brush and rub away over the entire body avoiding the face. We recommend wet body brushing as opposed to dry brushing.

🍃 **Exfoliants** Sea salt is an effective exfoliant. Use the finer salt rather than the course type. Once again you can add your chosen essential oils to enhance this full body treatment. Wet your entire body, then stand (if in the bath) or move out of the falling water (if in the shower) and rub all over with the salt blend. Your skin feels so clean and soft after this treatment, ready to accept your massage blend for the aromatic body rub!

🍃 **Relax and Slow Down** Most of us lead hectic busy lives. Taking time out can be a challenge for many but it is essential if you want to lead a more balanced life. A long bath, turning the television off and reading or getting back to nature by going for a nice walk can all do wonders for the soul. Prayer, meditation and gentle yoga stretches can help relax the mind and relieve tension in the body.

🍃 **Home Spa Products** There are some fantastic home spa products you can purchase now. Things like a foot spa or electric massager are all wonderful tools for your home spa. Health food stores or appliance stores will stock these. One of our favourites is the Galvanic Spa, a handheld device that delivers a Galvanic current to the skin, to stimulate cell renewal and encourage the absorption of key ingredients in your products by up to 70%. These devices make wonderful birthday or Christmas presents for your girlfriends.

🍃 **Getting a Good Night's Sleep** It seems the most natural thing to do to keep up with our fast-paced lives is to sacrifice sleep so we can cram more into our twenty-four hours. But slow down. Research is now suggesting that even if you miss only a few hours of shut-eye tonight, you are more likely to become ill tomorrow. On average, people spend 24 years of their lives asleep. Something that takes up that much time and is so closely linked to our immune systems must be one of the most important things for us to respect.

Whenever you feel ill or under the weather, the body's instant response is to want to sleep. There is a very good reason for this. Cytokines (immune system hormones) flood throughout the body when an infection is present and also act as a powerful sleep inducer, giving your body the chance to save energy and heal.

You know you are not getting enough sleep if you feel drowsy throughout the day, have a desire to sleep in, fall asleep within minutes of lying down, find it difficult to get up, are grumpy and irritable for no reason, feel emotional at the drop of a hat, need a cup of coffee first thing in the morning or doze off watching television at night!

To ensure you get a good night's sleep, get into positive healthy habits before taking yourself off to bed. Studies show that if you exercise regularly, you sleep better. Time spent in the outdoors also increases your ability to get a good night's sleep. Prepare the bedroom for sleep by lighting a vaporiser and placing two drops each of Lavender, Chamomile and Orange an hour before you are ready. Try not to watch television in bed, it may only stimulate you. Reading can do the same, although a lot of people find reading is a positive and helpful activity for a deep sleep! Do what works best for you.

If you are suffering from poor sleep avoid things like sugar, coffee, alcohol and other stimulants before bed (although our grandmothers may suggest a hot toddy is the best way to get off to sleep!). Try a warm milky drink before bed because it contains an enzyme called tryptophan, which induces sleep. Soothing classical music can help your nervous system to slow your heart rate, breathing and blood pressure. And according to research, lovemaking enhances the quality of sleep tenfold...!! Indeed.

Take Special Care Women are particularly good at giving, often putting their own needs last in order to support someone else, but we hope you can now see the importance of guilt-free indulgence and self care – each and every day! Having no time or money is no longer a valid excuse. Self care and real beauty is about making the best choices to help keep you afloat in this sometimes crazy world. The more you nurture and care for body and skin, the more aware you become of knowing how to support it. This is especially helpful if stress or illness strikes.

> You deserve the best, so treat yourself with the utmost respect and care. How you present yourself to the world reflects your own sensuality, beauty and spirit. Love the body you are in; groom it, nourish it, exercise it and pamper it, because when you do, you radiate an energy that is truly beautiful. And that is real beauty.

SuperWoman Survival

> **'Be an extraordinary human being without suffering SuperWoman Syndrome'**
> Kim Morrison & Fleur Whelligan

SuperWoman Syndrome – What Is It?

Eat well. Exercise. Don't get too fat. Don't get too skinny. Take time out. Relax. Work hard. Play often. Forge a career. Get business savvy. Travel the world. Keep the house clean. Bake homemade goodies. Expand yourself. Learn something new. Be a good mother. Be a great wife. Make time for friends. Smile often. Frown less. Volunteer…

Let's face it – it's a big call to be SuperWoman! To maintain it all and do it well can cause sheer exhaustion with symptoms like headaches, muscular aches and pains, anxiety, depression, irritability, inability to concentrate, and mood swings, now medically recognised as side effects of 'SuperWoman Syndrome' – a condition first named in the seventies.

As women struggle to balance multiple responsibilities, many wonder whatever happened to 'having it all'. How has life got so busy that there is little time left for me?

The truth is that being happy, healthy and the best you can be is all about commitment – a lasting commitment to a healthy, balanced lifestyle made up of the hundreds of small but important choices you make every day. But the million dollar question is: what is a healthy and balanced lifestyle in this sophisticated and fast-paced world? And how do you know if you really are making the best decisions about the way you live and what you do with your time?

At heart we all want to be healthy, successful and happy with ourselves, but many of us feel overwhelmed by information overload. The world around us is becoming more complex, technical and processed and filled with many more choices.

As authors and speakers, over the last 16 years we have heard women around the world asking for inspiration that will last a lifetime. They want a strategy for living with unbiased information they can rely upon when it comes to making everyday choices about business, their health and wellbeing and the welfare of their families. We are both passionate about our careers and our health, and this plea is close to our hearts; after all, finding a healthy balance is a challenge we face in our own lives as business women, mothers, wives and qualified health therapists!

Fortunately for us all, there is help. And if you break it down into manageable bits, it's not that hard. Remember though, everyone's experience of overload will be different, therefore the remedies will also vary. It is important to experiment and find the strategies and tools that work best for you. Maintaining balance is a lifetime process; it is a day-to-day journey of learning and gaining insight into how we can positively affect our health and relationships at work and in the home.

Beat SuperWoman Syndrome – Choose to Live at High Level Wellness

It's all very well and good saying 'choose to live at high-level wellness' – it's almost silly to suggest it! After all, we *all* want to live like that. The problem is, many people confuse 'wellness' with 'living without illness' rather than realising they have the power to live at an optimum level of health which positively affects every area of their life. So here are some top **LIPS Tips** to get you started on your journey. Don't try and achieve them all in one week; set yourself mini goals and work at implementing one of these strategies at a time into your life. The key then is to keep it going!

Prioritise and Delegate More Everywhere we go the two biggest excuses we hear from women for not taking care of themselves are not enough time or not enough money. In today's busy worlds, with such high financial and time pressures, it is easy to think they are valid excuses. We disagree.

It is not about time *or* money. We believe it is simply because you have not made yourself a priority. When was the last time you had a relaxation massage? If it was last week, congratulations! But it may have been months, even years since you had the pleasure. It may be that some of you are yet to enjoy that experience. If your reason for not having a massage recently is because you have not had enough time or money, is it really because you haven't had the time or money, or is it that you don't see this as a priority? Is it more a luxury than a necessity?

We believe the most important asset you have in your whole life is your health. A lot of you may find you put the needs of your partner, family or loved ones before your own. Women are *so* good at this. So if we suggested the health or lives of your children or partner depended on you having a massage this week – in other words, they would get sick if you didn't have one – would you find the time and money to do so? Of course you would. Your massage has now become a major priority.

Priorities are what drive us. They are our focus. If it was really important for you to have a holiday in Europe but you didn't have the time or money right now, you would start to make a plan. You would begin saving and begin to work out your itinerary. And whether it was one week or one year before you left, you would get there. You would get there because your holiday became a priority.

Many people have a great deal of trouble prioritising people and activities in their life. Think about yourself for a minute. Begin by assessing your relationships: Higher power, spouse/partner, children, friends, employment – is this your order of priority? Often people living with symptoms of SuperWoman Syndrome have this list reversed.

If you are really truthful, you'll admit that you believe no one else can do what you do. If you don't do things yourself they won't get done, everyone else is too busy, or you think you will be seen as a failure if you can't manage it all. Recognising that this way of thinking is not helping you is the first step, then learning to delegate and asking for help is next; however, learning to say 'no' at times could be your lifesaver too! Easier said than done, right?

Plan, Plan, Plan The key to managing a full-on busy life is to plan your day. Often we plan what we are doing for work but what about time out for you? What about your meals? Do you plan what you are going to eat for the day? What time will you fit in some exercise? When is your chill-out time? Read more on this in the Life Balance chapter.

Mothers – Manage Your Guilt For those of you who are mothers you will know what we are talking about. One of the toughest things for busy women who work is feeling comfortable about how much time they spend with their children. What is the right answer here – a full-time nanny, day care, half-days, a live-in au pair? The answer is: do what works for YOU and YOUR family. Our suggestion is that whatever decision you make, go with it, then limit the amount of guilt you allow yourself! (We know guilt won't completely go away, that's why we suggest a limit. Be kind to yourself.) And change it if it isn't working.

Something that worked for us (while the children were all preschoolers) was that we shared a nanny. It was cost-effective because she looked after the four children in one home while we worked in the other. Then, while we were writing our books, we often worked from 5-7am (before the children woke up) or 8pm midnight (once they were in bed). If you really want to achieve something, you make it a priority and do what works. Just remember, your health is number one priority here so if you are going to push yourself for a time you may need to supplement with high quality vitamins, minerals and antioxidants and take extra time for things like massages, to sleep on weekends and exercise. The most important thing is to ensure you take care of yourself – after all, those babes are going to need you firing on all cylinders when you are with them!

Good Food, Good Mood You have heard it all before and yet again we reinforce it. Eat fresh, whole foods. Choose live foods (as nature intended) and avoid processed/packaged foods as much as possible. When writing our book it was mind-blowing how much fantastic information there was out there to substantiate this. What is important is that you truly get 'you are what you eat'. What goes into your mouth has an effect on how you think and feel, your energy levels, your mood, and your productivity. *(Read Cyndi's chapter thoroughly)* We are all passionate about this important topic and yet it is often one of the last things busy women think about. Eating on the run, eating packaged foods, takeaways, muffins and coffee or, worse still, having no time to eat at all, are typical SuperWoman Syndrome habits. Trust us – if you do not invest in your health and wellbeing now, then sickness will invest itself in you later.

Role Models Not Supermodels We love that saying, 'Role Models not Super Models'. It's a very powerful message particularly at this time when advertising and marketing is so based on the 'beauty' images of rail-thin and very tall models! What tone of voice do you use when discussing your health and wellbeing? How do you talk about your body, hair and skin? How do you accept compliments? How do you talk around your friends and family?

Most women will agree they don't want their children growing up with hang-ups about their body or image, but if they hear their role models and mentors saying things like 'I hate my hair', 'I'm so fat', 'I can't be bothered', 'Money doesn't grow on trees you know' 'I'm so broke' – then what messages are we giving them?

When a child asks for a certain toy for example and you cannot afford it – is this what you tell them? 'Money doesn't grow on trees you know'. Or do you try to encourage them by saying, 'Wow that would be amazing; do you think we could come up with a plan to save up so you can get that toy?' You are not saying 'no' are you? And the responsibility is now on them to be creative. You are helping them see they can achieve goals if they create a plan. Suggestions like this can empower children (and SuperWomen!) remarkably. *(Check out Jodie's chapters for excellent financial guidance.)*

Age Gracefully Ageing is a natural biological process we experience as each year passes. Sadly, women often berate themselves as they age – almost as if they associate more wrinkles with less value. They turn to expensive *ANTI*-ageing products, or the more radical options – non-invasive surgical procedures (Botox) or surgery! Now, while it is important to pamper yourself and use good skincare, your intention should be to nourish and care for your skin and body to help it age gracefully, rather than engaging in a war with the wrinkles. If we place a greater emphasis on reducing stress, eating a healthy diet with plenty of water, fresh air, skin protection and regular exercise, along with plenty of sleep and relaxation, then we give our body the best chance to age in a more graceful way. There's a better chance you will enjoy the ride too!

Remember, age is just a number. Laughter lines, fine lines – even frown lines – characterise who we are. They do not mean it's time to go under the surgeon's knife. We have met women of all ages (wrinkles 'n' all!) who radiate energy, vitality and beauty. Growing older is growing wiser; life is about loving yourself and accepting who you are. A healthy attitude is the key here. It plays a significant role in how you regard yourself and others. For more information go to our website www.creativewellbeing.com for more natural alternatives to ageing gracefully.

Daily Body Treat How would you feel if we told you we both have a full body massage every day? Well, it's true, and we have been having these massages every day for the past sixteen years; not once have we missed a day! It is the ultimate skin treatment. We love it and cannot imagine life without it.

You may well be aware of the benefits of massage. Massage increases circulation, promotes sleep, reduces stress levels, increases muscle tone, promotes elimination of toxins and waste, supports weight loss, increases skin elasticity and enhances wellbeing – to name but a few. Imagine if you could do this every day. Well, every one of you SuperWomen out there can, and it only takes a few minutes every morning.

Having a daily full body rub or massage is another great insurance policy for your overall health. The important thing to remember is to ensure the products you massage your body with are natural and full of essential vitamins and minerals. Also, it is important to make sure this is a good body rub or polish, not some airy-fairy tickle! You want your body to wake up, feel alive and be ready to get into your day.

You may have guessed by now that your daily body massage is performed by YOU! The daily body massage happens after your morning shower, before you get dressed. (Ideally you have done your morning exercise programme.)

Once you pat yourself dry choose three Aromatherapy essential oils to support you throughout the day. You may have a long, full-on day ahead so it is important to choose oils that are going to be uplifting and enduring like Rosemary, Lemon, Peppermint, Sandalwood, Lime or Basil. Or, if you are feeling a little run down or tired, go for healing, stimulating oils like Tea Tree, Eucalyptus, Pine, Lemongrass, Rosemary or Orange. If your skin is dry and looking as if it needs some good nutrition, then choose the skin-active oils Frankincense, Rose, Petigrain, Rosewood, Geranium or Bergamot.

It is important that you choose a high quality cold pressed carrier oil and then add three essential oils that you like. The most wonderful thing about choosing your three essential oils is the fact that you are asking yourself every morning, 'How do I feel?' Normally we are so busy getting everyone else ready or thinking about what we have to do for the day ahead that we forget the most important thing of all – and that is you. Acknowledging your body like this every morning is a powerful way to set yourself up for a great day.

How do you feel when you stand naked in front of a mirror? Are you horrified, pleased, shocked or rapt? If you cannot stand in front of the mirror every morning and say 'Wow – I look and feel great', then you definitely need to take on the daily body massage routine! We are often quick to criticise our bodies, be disappointed in it and abuse it – literally! Now is the beginning of the rest of your life and it is time to acknowledge the amazing machine that houses *you*. Your body is a temple, an incredible vehicle that transports you through life, no matter how it looks. We can guarantee there are people out there who would love to have your problem areas rather than theirs. Just remember, it's ok to want to change your body, but do it with better health as your goal rather than focusing on weight loss or shape change. If the focus is on feeling better, there are fewer chances of disappointment when certain weight or size measurements are not achieved. Give yourself time to change if that is what you would like to have happen. Don't expect miracle creams or surgery to 'fix' you. A daily body massage will have you honouring and nurturing your body before you know it, and *then* you will see transformations unfold before your eyes! The focus is better health, not your size.

It doesn't really matter how you massage your body in the morning as long as you go from head to toe or toe to head, do all over, and really wake your body up. We tend to start at the toes and work our way up each leg, into the tummy region in a clockwise direction to support digestive functions, up over the chest and shoulders, across the lower back, buttocks and tops of thighs. Here is a good place to give an extra special rub to increase circulation and help remove any cellulite (you know that dimply orange peel look that we cover successfully with clothing but can't seem to hide in a bikini!) that tends to build in this region. Work as far as you can up the back and across the shoulder blades, then rub each arm, forearm and hand, up across the shoulders and then finish with nice gentle strokes into your neck. Complete your massage by pressing both hands onto your face and taking a couple of nice, deep breaths. It would have taken you longer to read this then do it.

This is one of the loveliest things you can do for yourself and it really is simple, effective and not at all time consuming.

Often we do our morning body rubs with two children copying our every move and wanting their own oil-blends. (For children, use only one drop of essential oil in the carrier oil). It is such a healthy fun way to start your day and what great modelling for your children to see the importance you place on your body's welfare.

We challenge you to take this morning ritual on and invite you to let us know how you are feeling after three weeks. Everyone we have met who has done this for the full 21 days has become committed for life. And your skin will feel fantastic! You will have no dry skin on your body but, more than that, you will feel better on the inside. You will feel special, nurtured and energised.

Good Mood Oils

Essential oils have the ability to work on an emotional level too. If you are not sure which oils to choose for your daily body rub, then try one of these combinations to boost your mood and change any negative feelings.

> Pre Menstrual – Clary Sage, Geranium, Orange
> Tired – Rosemary, Lemon, Basil
> Emotionally vulnerable – Rose, Geranium, Sandalwood
> Angry – Bergamot, Ylang Ylang, chamomile
> Anxious – Neroli, Lavender, Frankincense
> Depressed – Clary Sage, Lime, Geranium
> Negative – Geranium, Lime, Clary Sage
> Unfeminine – Rose, Neroli, Jasmine
> Stressed – Chamomile, Geranium, Rosewood

Taking Care of the SUPERWOMAN in You!

We know what it means to have little time. We know what it is like to have no extra money to take time and indulge ourselves when we really want to or need to. But we have discovered that 'no time' or 'no money' is no longer a valid excuse for not taking care of ourselves.

Women are incredibly good at giving. They often put their own needs last in order to support or help someone else. We are suggesting you start to make yourself a priority. Take a bit of time out for you. Make it guilt-free and savour it. Face it -no one else will do it for you! There is only one person you can count on to do this and that is YOU. Just think about it for a moment – if you did pay a little more time and attention to your own needs, how would that look? What would it feel like? Taking a few moments at the end of a busy day to run a bath, put on some music and light a candle is not a huge ask or expense. Using a natural exfoliant on your hands and painting your nails does wonders for how you feel about yourself, and a facial steam helps your skin glow and your mind unwind. All of these treats take little time or money.

We are no different from you or the countless other women out there trying to do their best. We just make it a priority to indulge ourselves at least once a day with some of the things we have talked about here. We have also realized how important it is to the welfare of our husbands, children, friends, family and work colleagues that we do take care. After all, when the woman of the house is happy and healthy life runs pretty smoothly for everyone around her!

Prioritising your physical and emotional wellness is the key to a truly happy and vibrant life. Taking responsibility has a ripple effect, positively enhancing the lives of everyone around you. Treat yourself with the utmost respect and be grateful for where you are, right here, right now. Know you have the power to be an extraordinary human being without suffering SuperWoman Syndrome. It is about feeling good in your own skin, being proud of who you are and who you are becoming. You are an amazing SuperWoman and you deserve the best!

Get Your Body Moving

> *The excuse for not exercising is usually that we are too tired: Did you know that lack of exercise IS the actual reason why we are tired in the first place?*
> Kim Morrison and Fleur Welligan

The human body was designed to be active and *MOVE*. You cannot achieve optimum health and vitality if you are sedentary – no matter how good your diet is! Physical activity supports all your body functions – it strengthens your heart and lungs, builds strong healthy muscles and gives you that wonderful sense of wellbeing as your brain releases 'feel good' endorphins each time you exercise. At the end of the day it doesn't matter how you move your body as long as you move it!

But it's *so* easy to make excuses not to exercise. There seem to be so many distractions and other more important matters that need our attention (this is especially so for those suffering SuperWoman Syndrome!) It's understandable that all these excuses pop up. After all, life is so busy. The reality is, things will always pop up, and you will always be able to find a 'valid' excuse – if you want to. *A commitment to your health is a priority.* If you want to be a *healthy* SuperWoman then plan ways of exercising that can easily be integrated into your busy life. Make sure it is something you enjoy and stick with it. For those of you who detest the thought of exercising (we know you are out there!) then make sure you do something like walk, swim or cycle for 20-30 minutes at least 3 times a week. Find ways of exercising that you can enjoy and stick with it until a habit is formed. This is usually about 28 days on average.

Trust us here – the endorphins released will boost your immunity and increase your level of health and wellbeing. Ask anyone who exercises how much better they feel for doing so. It's a given! You have to make time!

The topic of exercise is as big as nutrition. It can also be as confusing. We are constantly bamboozled by the latest exercise gadget or fad. The exercise industry is as much a moneymaking phenomenon as the food one. But at the end of the day it doesn't matter how you move your body as long as you are moving it! It is interesting when we both look at our own exercise routines. Both of us love to be outdoors and enjoy walking. We both love exercising but in completely different ways. Kim has always been very active and competitive; she has played most sports with particular interests in netball and tennis (which she stills play socially today). She has also run in ultramarathon events where she had the honor of representing Australia when she lived in Melbourne. Kim loves going to the gym regularly and has competed in a body sculpting competition.

Fleur on the other hand is not so competitive. She feels exercise should be a fun way to get the body moving. It has to be something she enjoys doing that makes her feels vibrant and energised afterwards. One of Fleur's biggest loves is to crank up the stereo in the morning and get on the re-bounder for at least 20 minutes. One of her other passions is to dance. Fleur and her husband Dave love Ceroc dancing; to them it is a brilliant form of exercise. Fleur did join a gym for a while but as she confesses the only real reason she went there was because they had such brilliant showers!

We have spoken to many people about physical activity, and for the majority of them exercising on a regular basis is one of life's toughest challenges. We keep wondering what magic formula we could come up with that would make people commit to working out. What would have them stick to their New Years resolution or maintain a simple program regularly? What works for some may not work for others, and if one day you feel great about exercising, chances are there will be some days you don't. It is a challenge for many, but it is an investment for your overall health. The harsh reality is you can't pop a magic herbal pill and voila it is done! And for those of you wishing it, unfortunately no one else can do it for you either!

Your emotional health and physical health are very strongly linked. To be fit emotionally gives you the edge to support yourself through your physical health journey. Put it simply with a positive attitude you can overcome any self sabotage or negativities towards exercise.

Because we know there are different personality types out there (check out Allison's Who Am I Who Are You chapter on page 31) we have devised a couple of different ways to get your daily dose of fitness. There is the 45E (45minute Endurance), the 20I (the 20minute Intensity) and the Fab4 In5 (4 exercises performed daily in just 5minutes) —they are all detailed in full at our website www.creativewellbeing.com In the scheme of your whole day none of them take much time. It's a small effort for a huge reward and you can move your way towards a healthier, fitter, more toned body simply. Now that's got to be a good thing!

And if you need a real reason why, then here are twenty top reasons to get your body moving. We might be stating the obvious here, but unless you are prepared to get up off your butt and commit to some form of regular exercise regime for life then you might as well just skip this chapter all together. But if you choose to do that...don't ever complain that you are not happy with your body, state of health or physical appearance! If you don't exercise and eat well you have absolutely no right!

> *To know a person's experience from the past, examine the body now. To know a person's body in the future, examine their experiences now.*
> Deepak Chopra

LIPS tips for getting your body moving.

🌿 **Energy Levels Rise and You Feel Better.** If people only realised that their excuse for not exercising, because they are too tired, is the reason they are tired in the first place! Exercise increases your energy levels. You may not necessarily feel like doing it, but once you have completed your workout for the day, the feel-good factor kicks in and there is an increase in oxygen levels. People who exercise regularly notice their energy levels are a lot higher. You may have heard some people actually get a buzz out of exercising. Hard to believe maybe, but research is showing that the body really does experience that 'high' after exercise.

🌿 **Being Active Improves Mental Wellbeing.** When the stresses of life increase, your job is getting on top of you, or the kids have become too much, then go out for some fresh air and get your body moving. Either join a club that has crèche facilities or roster with your partner to take turns. Maybe try going to the gym or for a walk in your lunch hour instead of sitting in the lunch room. Even doing a lap around the outside of your house can do wonders for a stressed mind. Trust us – we have done this when the kids were small!

🌿 **You Have Fun and Associate with Like-Minded People.** Exercising with friends can be a great way to catch up. Going for a walk or cycle together instead of meeting for coffee has many health benefits. For those of you who struggle to stay committed to exercise, having a buddy is a good way to keep accountable and focused. Being more active, research suggests, increases self-esteem and confidence, and you are likely to hang out with people with similar attitudes.

🌿 **You Can Eat More Without Gaining Weight.** Regular exercisers tend to have more nutritional needs than non-exercisers. Plus, they tend to be able to eat more without making a difference to their weight, as their metabolic rate is higher. Research suggests you don't crave sugar or fatty foods as much when exercising regularly either, so all round it's good for the waistline!

🌀 **Weight Is Likely To Stay Off.** Did you know that most people who lose weight find it again within one to two years? One of the reasons for this is: they don't exercise and stick to healthy eating. It has been stated that 95 percent of people who have lost weight keep it off, *if they exercise regularly and eat well.*

🌀 **Your Posture Improves.** As your abdominal and back muscles get stronger, you walk more like an athlete! Your back lengthens, you feel taller. You are less prone to injury, and good posture helps breathing, flexibility, blood flow and energy levels.

🌀 **Exercise Helps Maintain or Increase Flexibility.** Those who exercise and stretch have a much better range of movement and flexibility. This is helpful in maintaining the daily tasks you need to perform like bending over to pick up things, sweeping the floor or reaching for something up high. Being more flexible also reduces the risk of injury.

🌀 **Exercise Promotes Sleep.** It has been proven many times that those who exercise regularly fall asleep more quickly and sleep longer with fewer interruptions. This can be due to hormone changes and the fact the body is more relaxed and prepared for rest after exercise.

🌀 **Exercise Helps Eliminate Toxins.** By increasing blood flow through exercise you also increase the lymphatic flow. Lymph flows at a much slower rate than blood – around one twentieth the pace. The lymphatic system helps eliminate toxins from the body and when it is functioning well, you have less chance of storing toxins, holding water, suffering from body odour, storing excess weight, having a sluggish bowel or problem skin.

🌀 **Disuse is Disaster.** You only have to immobilise a limb for three to four hours before the muscles start to atrophy, that is why you wriggle and move in your sleep (sometimes, it is said) hundreds of times a night. Your body was designed to *move*.

🌀 **Body Movement Increases Oxygen Levels.** The more sedentary you become, the less oxygen your body utilises. The less oxygen you have available, the more slug-like you become and the more your brain, muscles and organs are depleted. The less active you are, the harder it is for your heart to pump blood around your body, so the more you avoid exercise, chances are you'll feel more sluggish, carry more weight and feel less vital. This is because you have reduced the essential oxygen and nutrient levels in your body. *Being active increases the oxygen levels in your body.*

Inactive Muscles Shrink. The old 'use it or lose it' theory. If muscles are not exercised or used regularly there is much less blood flow, much less oxygen and therefore less vitality. When muscles shrink they lose their strength and tone and this lessens their ability to support and move you. *Move your muscles so they can move you!*

Exercise Increases Bone Strength and Density. Without continuous resistance exercise, bones can weaken and thin. Bones are unable to form new bone matrix and as a result of this (along with poor nutrition), you are more likely to develop conditions like osteoporosis. Research shows that people who exercise more regularly decrease their chances of bone diseases.

Exercise Improves Bowel Function. Lack of regular exercise can disrupt bowel function and impair the digestive system regardless of what you eat. There is research suggesting you should eliminate every time you eat. A scary thought if you are a grazer as opposed to a two- or three-meals-a-day person! A good healthy aim is to have at least one bowel motion a day. There could be a bowel dysfunction if this is not the case for you. Get moving and your bowel will too!

Exercise Means a Good Strong Pulse. Generally speaking, an active, healthy person will have a good resting pulse (heart rate) of around 60-70 beats per minute. An inactive person can show resting rates of 80-90 beats per minute. High performance athletes can possess resting heart rates of around 30-40 beats per minute. Yours may be on the low side due to being fit or if you are genetically predisposed to a lower rate. Your pulse may be on the high side if you are nervous, on medication, stressed or drinking things like coffee or alcohol. As you increase your exercise levels your resting pulse (heart rate) usually drops, meaning it is becoming more efficient, so your heart does not have to work as hard to pump the blood around your body. An efficient heart means a healthier body. (To check your heart rate (pulse) place your first two fingers on the opposite inside wrist, next to ligaments, until you find the pulsating pump. Count the number of beats for 15 seconds, then multiply by 4. That is your resting heart rate.)

Blood Pressure Remains More Constant. Blood pressure is a measurement of how open your blood vessels are. A lower number means your heart doesn't have to work as hard to pump the blood through the blood vessels. A normal blood pressure for a healthy adult is around 120/80; however research suggests you should be aiming to lower even this. Figures of around 145/95 are considered to be hypertension (high blood pressure). People who exercise regularly reduce the risk of developing heart-threatening conditions like hypertension (high blood pressure) by nearly a third. Appropriate regular exercise may also help lower blood pressure in those who already suffer from high blood pressure. Stress, poor nutrition, lack of or too much exercise, medication, illness, caffeine, alcohol, nerves and adrenaline can all affect blood pressure.

Exercise Makes Your Heart Fit. Your heart is a muscle. The more you exercise this muscle the fitter and stronger it gets. Cardio exercise like walking, running, cycling, swimming, dancing etc. increases your heart rate which tones and strengthens your heart muscle. The fitter and stronger your heart, the more able it is to pump blood around your body, so the better your health and wellbeing.

You Save Money You may spend money on a good pair of running shoes, a health club membership, athletic clothing or yoga classes, (oh how girls love to shop!) but in the long run you will spend less on doctor's bills and prescriptions – exercise expenses should definitely be seen as an investment, rather than a cost.

How to test your heart rate when exercising

If you have ever been to a gym or had a full medical test then you may have had your target heart rate (THR) tested. It is a test that evaluates your heart rate when working at less than your maximum effort. The test is normally measured around 75-85% of your maximum heart rate (MHR). A test that goes beyond this should only ever be performed with a qualified doctor or physician. To work out your target heart rate, use this equation:

220 - Your age = Maximum Heart Rate
(MHR) MHR x 75-85% = Target Heart Rate (THR)

Exercise Lowers Cholesterol. Cholesterol generally gets a pretty bad rap even though it is essential for a healthy body. Most of your cholesterol is manufactured within your body by your liver, but you can also get it from animal foods like meat, poultry, fish, eggs and dairy products. No plants contain cholesterol. The important thing to know is that there are two types: LDL – low-density lipoprotein (which is the bad one) and HDL – high-density lipoprotein (which is the good one). High LDL levels are caused by diets loaded with degraded and processed foods. Research suggests sedentary people are more likely to have higher levels of cholesterol, therefore increasing the risk of cardiovascular disease.

You May Reduce Your Risk of Cancer. There seems to be truckloads of research and information on this topic. We read books by some authors who stated they had conclusive evidence to support the argument that exercise reduces your chances of cancer, and others who agreed, but did not feel there was enough evidence to prove it. Regardless, both sides say exercise improves your chances of not getting cancer of any kind. It's got to be worth doing!

No more excuses girls – to be an extraordinary Super Woman - you have to get up off your butts and get that tush moving!

How to achieve your WEALTH goals

Disclaimer: The information contained in the wealth chapters is for general information only and is not specific to your individual needs.

Accordingly, it should not be acted upon without reference to your personal information and financial adviser.

The Truth On Wealth

Jodie McIver

> *"The real measure of your wealth is how much you'd be worth if you lost all your money."*
> Anonymous

What Does Being Wealthy Really Mean?

According to the dictionary 'wealthy' means having an abundant supply of money and or possessions of value. What I find quite disconcerting is that the vast majority of people make an almost immediate connection between wealth and money and forget about the possessions of value including things like health, spiritual life, family, loved ones and friends.

Our society has been cultured to measure wealth and success this way. I believe it is whatever you want it to be, and counting dollars and judging in terms of job, house, car, clothes and lifestyle are viewed by mainstream society as the signs for gauging wealth – is a fairly shallow way of just keeping up with the Joneses so to speak. Not only is this accepted in society; parents, educators, colleagues and peers seem to encourage it.

Research strongly indicates that in fact money and happiness have very little in common. After many years in the finance industry, I am inclined to agree with them. Wealthy people are assumed to be very happy and yet there are countless examples where money and true wealth aren't related. In that case, being financially wealthy might buy you a better class of misery! When you think about Mother Teresa and Princess Diana, who lived more on their own terms? What is a true and accurate picture of wealth for you?

Whilst my passion and commitment to achieving financial success is paramount, I believe that a true indicator of wealth is when someone on their deathbed can genuinely say they have lived life on their terms – that they have lived a `contented, *fulfilled, challenged existence*'. That they have enjoyed life, have few regrets and have done most of the things they wanted to do. Financially though, I believe success is when you have enough investments, making you enough money (withstanding all market conditions) to live the lifestyle you would like. For some people, that might be $80,000 a year. For others, $80,000 wouldn't even cut their monthly requirement! It is a number that is completely appropriate and relevant to you.

Throughout this chapter there will be some LIPS tips with tasks associated with them and whilst you are reading this chapter I would like to suggest you do your tasks as you go. So here it is ladies, your number one task.

LIPS TIP: Get a Wealth and Prosperity Journal Your journal doesn't have to be fancy; it can be whatever size you like. Then write down what you would clearly define as 'wealth' and what being wealthy means to you. I then want you to consider linking an income level that facilitates living on your own terms.

If you could click your fingers and have the life you want, right now, what would it look like? Take a minute to consider that…if there were no limitations, how would your life be? Write it all down.

> *So... if your life does not look like this picture you have painted right now what's stopping you?*

Prosperity Mindset

The start of all good intentions is to have the right attitude. By reading this LIPS book, you have started on the right track – you can't help but have a fantastic attitude and most definitely create good intention when reading it. Now in order to achieve your definition of wealth we need to achieve a basic understanding and knowledge of your finances and the follow through with a good plan. The next two chapters are designed to give you a snap shot into the world of wealth creation, how to get out of financial woes if you are in them and how to implement a plan with quick tips along the way to make it fun and simple to do.

Being wealthy is every person's living right, but achieving wealth is not always as easy for most people. Whilst planning your financial future is paramount, you also need to be able to enjoy life in the meantime.... to live NOW! Often, that is the hardest part of working out where to start.

There is so much to tell you about making money that I am sure I could fill many books, let alone a few chapters! The purpose of this chapter is not to bombard you with heaps of technical financial terms and jargon. It is also not for the astute investor who I am sure would practice a lot of what I am outlining here. It is for the person who is keen to learn, implement ways to create wealth and work out a plan to get ahead... basically, for anyone who wants to start taking control of their money instead of their money (or lack of it) controlling them!

Are you limiting yourself?

Are you limiting yourself with negative self-talk or thoughts? If you tell your brain 'that something can't be done,' then it believes you, and the search for an appropriate answer ends. Your mind doesn't even try and work out the best way to get there or find a solution....it simply stops thinking about it....are you limiting yourself by not allowing your mind to explore and dream? You can't really lie to yourself – go on, indulge in 'what if' and start imagining the endless possibilities.

Let's start at the beginning. What are you trying to achieve financially? Are you limiting yourself by negative thoughts about how it can't be done, I can't afford it, I am broke etc etc...? Just stop for a minute and concentrate on some positive thoughts about what you want in life, no matter how far-fetched or extravagant. All too often positive thinking works because the 'thinker' dwells on the positive thought...simple.

These days our lives are so fast-paced and consuming, so it seems the easy path to concentrate on is the negatives of your life, especially if you aren't aware of the tools or processes available to change it. The basis of all change comes from the desire and the will to make a difference. Even small changes like reduced spending and financial structure can make a monumental difference to the rest of your life going forward.

You have to want it – imagine it – please don't limit yourself. A lot of people are good at limiting themselves and their future. I am sure you have huge talent, ambition, intelligence and a whole host of other good qualities...but do you perform below your potential? Some fundamental flaws in negative thinking often result in mediocrity....take a moment to consider the following;

- Do you place limits on yourself that limit your potential, high level performance and success?

- Do you lack the realisation that you create your own circumstances?

- Do you accept your lot in life, as 'just the way it is' or 'I made my bed now I lie in it'?

- Have a fear of change or new, unknown things.

- Don't take responsibility for your actions - making excuses, cynicism, blaming others or circumstances, unreasonable litigious claims etc.

- Suffer Tall Poppy Syndrome - cutting successful people down to bring them back to a lower level.

- Attempt to please everyone.

- Find it hard to say 'no'.

- Have a tendency to believe what you see or hear from others or through the media without checking the facts.

- Try to make everything and everyone fit to your outlook on life.

- Try to mould yourself to what you think others approve of.

- Use words like, 'But', 'I wish' and 'that would be nice'

Humans naturally put numerous self-imposed constraints on themselves. They almost always put a ceiling or limitation on what they believe they can do. If a person is physically capable of 100 push-ups but they believe they can only do ten, then ten is how many they will generally do. Moving beyond these limitations is a critical element in achieving the best possible financial result.

> *"Keep away from people who try to belittle your ambition. Small people always do that, but the really great make you feel that you, too, can become great."*
> *Mark Twain*

Sometimes individuals will just fall into line with the majority and conform to the standards set by others without questioning things from their own belief system.

There is an old quote, 'popular opinion is usually wrong'. A popular opinion is formed by the majority, and the majority is usually misinformed. Hence the need for accurate education.

Add to that the principal that most people don't challenge or question the status quo, they don't look at things from a different perspective – they just blindly follow the leader and display 'herd mentality' in their lives.

LIPS Tip: See which way the crowd is going, and go the other way! By following the 'herd mentality' you are setting yourself up for failure. Remember, the majority of the population is not very wealthy. Be bold, educate yourself so you are not misinformed and then be mindful of the negative ways of thinking so that you can take control, begin to change and have the most amazing, successful life you would dare to dream.

> *"Patterning your life around other's opinions is nothing more than slavery."*
> Lawana Blackwell,
> The Dowry of Miss Lydia Clark, 1999

By starting the learning process you are unlocking those limitations. Chances are you are not in a position to make it real for you now, and you may even feel uncertain whether you can create it in the future. But it will lead to two key factors that may make the world of difference - personal growth and financial freedom.

Education And Learning

Let me explain briefly who I am, where I have come from and why I believe you can achieve financial success if you put your mind to it.

I have worked in the financial industry for over 12 years now, I am in my early 30s and at the time of writing this book am pregnant with my first child. I have a partner (fiancée actually!) Peter, who is a great man, my number one supporter, and my best mate. Part of being successful, I believe, is having a good team of supporters around you, whether it is your partner, someone in your family or a couple of key friends. You want people who will be positive and give great encouragement. But if you find there are some who bring you down, discourage you and knock your goals and dreams then perhaps you need to 'divorce' them (I mean that figuratively of course!)

After my education, I started working in law firms with the intention of studying law. My mum is a lawyer and had always been in this industry, so the time I spent after school washing dishes and licking stamps in the law office must have conditioned me to think this was what I wanted too. It wasn't until I moved to the city to seek fame and fortune that my path suddenly changed I was offered an Adviser Assistant role in a financial planning firm.

At that time, anything associated with money and finance eluded me. My credit card was always maxed out and I barely had enough money to pay the rent, let alone fuel my little car. Being in my late teens and early 20's, nightclubs and partying were more of a priority than food, and I certainly never thought about saving money, only about how to survive until the next pay day.

But slowly, in my new role as an assistant to a financial adviser, I started to learn about money, savings and financial planning. I met some really influential people who seemed to have their life so together. Something clicked inside. I started studying finance at night while I worked full time. I often say I would like to follow in my grandmother's footsteps, she believed at 75 we should still be learning something new every day!

This new finance environment didn't change my spending habits at first, but the learning certainly gave me direction and goals. Surrounding myself with goal oriented, successful people helped hugely!

The man I was in a relationship with at the time became my husband. We spent the next few years struggling with a mortgage, mounting bills and we always seemed to live beyond our means. Even though I worked in the industry, I still hadn't really 'got it'. We had insurances and small investments but because there was always a shortfall of cash flow, everything felt challenged.

I never really understood the importance of budgeting and goal-setting in relation to 'making money' back then. When my marriage broke down, we sold everything and split the proceeds in half. I took my share of what was left, and when reality sunk in that I was on my own, I got serious about my future.

Since that time I truly believe I have been on a path of self discovery, constantly learning, maturing and meeting new people. But the main thing I achieved was learning to budget!

If you can take one thing from this chapter about making money – it is first and foremost learning to budget! You have probably seen the statistics. The majority of people aren't wealthy, and one of the main reasons why the majority of people aren't wealthy is because they don't budget!

As I developed ways to budget and learn where my money was going, I also learned to use the banks money to make money. I learned to invest in good quality assets. I basically started from nothing all over again. I used to think all debt was bad but now I can certainly appreciate there is such a thing as good debt and bad debt. Now, if I can do it from scratch and learn these basic fundamentals, then I believe anyone can!

Most people I see in my daily life as a financial adviser come to me with a legacy. Often, they have had negative experiences with finances (and financial planners!) and don't know where to begin. I believe the best place to begin the process is to really learn about the basics. Understanding the key parts to making money and applying them to your situation is what works. The focus really should be about learning the fundamentals and then you will be in a position to make decisions about 'your' future and not just blindly trusting any one person with your hard-earned money.

This doesn't mean that you need to spend hours researching or analysing the property or stockmarket; what it does mean is that you need to make the commitment to investigate the best possible way to maximise your existing situation and put a plan in place to move that forward. This begins with education. I will try to outline some strategies you can implement yourselves, but the best way is to find someone (preferably a good adviser) who can outline the fundamentals of investment, income and taxation and will show you how to apply this to your situation...like a partner in life but for your financial affairs. Just like a great athlete needs a great coach, so a good financial future needs a specialist coach to assist in your journey – it's a smart thing to do – just don't give away your power to make decisions about your future.

Learning and education is really the key element and the place where we begin.

The fundamentals of wealth creation are easy to learn and the first key part is to change your focus on becoming a capitalist – that is, someone who earns income from assets rather than from personal exertion. Imagine being able to retire (early or when 'you' want) and live off the income your assets produce, rather than being forced to accept the Centrelink Age Pension of $13,000 each plus some small extra benefits in retirement.

The amount of capital you have now (property etc), or can amass, with conventional savings and investment programs (including retirement) are unlikely to be sufficient to fulfill your needs and will almost certainly not fulfill your wants – either now or in your well earned retirement.

Humans have the capacity to think strategically and tactically. Put simply, strategic is big picture, tactical is daily chores and details. Approximately 90% of people have that tactical strength – they are busy working, busy paying bills, busy doing household chores, just busy 'existing'. The challenge is getting that strategic, big picture view at the best of times....which is impossible when you are immersed in the distractions and details of the day-to-day stuff like work, home, whatever is happening in your world right now. We tend to fall into the trap of just going through the motions, day in, day out. It is a classic case of not seeing the forest for the trees.

Usually a person's strategic view of their life can fit on the back of a postage stamp. You really need to stand back from your situation and clearly identify what's truly important.

After considering the strategic view of your finances, adopting the right attitude, then comes.... understanding 'that anything worthwhile takes time'. Think about some of the successes in your life -career, family, education. Did they happen overnight? Think about team sports. Do most teams automatically become champions overnight or does it take months and years to develop winning strategies? Do you obtain university degrees overnight? Have a baby straight after conception? From your personal relationships with family and friends, to education, in business and in play...anything worthwhile takes time. That is not to say the process cannot be stepped up a few notches. As we continue in these chapters, I will endeavour to educate and provide tools for you to enhance your knowledge of the financial maze so you can effectively

So how can you make money work for you rather than you work for money, in order to have the freedom to do what you want to do? Imagine you are driving somewhere...you have a map, the car but no idea where you are going! You really need to have a direction when considering where you want to go with your finances. No point in having the road map if you don't know where you want to drive to. The following advice is to give you an idea of how to make a start in the direction for yourself. But let's first talk about debt.

Good Debt Bad Debt

I have mentioned two types of debt, good and bad. Good debt is any debt used for an 'income producing' asset and is 'tax deductible' such as investment loans for houses (not the home you live in) and shares, business loans etc. Bad debt is extremely common and is all debt used for consumption or private use such as home loans, car loans, credit cards and store cards. This is the debt we must try and eliminate pay back as soon as possible! Let's take a closer look at how we can do that.

3 Steps To Financial Freedom

> 'The fundamentals of wealth creation are easy to learn and the first key part is to change your focus on becoming a capitalist – that is, someone who earns income from assets rather than from personal exertion'
> **Jodie McIver**

There are countless books written about making money, financial planning, becoming wealthy or financially free. Most of these outline key concepts such as creating budgets and paying yourself first – this is sound advice and forms the basis for future planning. Let me explain the easiest way to begin.

Three critical steps to financial freedom

Step 1: Create a Budget/Spending Plan

Step 2: Expenses - Identify leftover money or a shortfall – if surplus, move onto step 3, if shortfall go to part on 'Smart Strategies to Exit Bad Debt' and take action!

Step 3: Money Makes Money -Take advantage of the leftover money. Go to the part on 'Using Money to Make Money' to create a strategic plan to invest wisely

Budgets / Spending Plans

Oh groan! I know, no-one particularly likes hearing the word 'budget' but it is seriously the only place to start. There is no point wishing to becoming financially well off if you don't make an effort to understand what is happening to the money you are earning now! Ask anyone who is financially happy and they will be able to tell you where ALL of their money is and where it goes each month!

A classic example is employees who recall in horror every July when they get their Group Certificate 'did I really earn that much, where did it all go?' This is something I hear all the time and is generally because there has been little or no budget planning.

One of the most common things that can **limit your capacity** to reach aspired goals is 'insufficient funds' – either in savings, surplus income or asset equity.

Most people think budgets are negative and indicate 'deprivation'; however it is just a 'spending plan' that allows you to make decisions on where to better spend your hard earned money. We know that we need to eventually become 'capitalists' (ie. instead of you working, your money works to provide your income) so right now we need to establish if you have a surplus each month or a deficit. If the idea of throwing away money or living beyond your means makes you (or your partner) happy, then of course, do it. If not, then you need to work out areas in your 'spending plan' to give you freedom to enjoy your lifestyle or the freedom to start planning for your future.

'Budget' is the correct term for your list of 'money coming in' and 'money going out' and is like outlining a profit and loss statement for your household. People get into trouble when they have more money going out than they have coming in! Living beyond your means won't make you wealthy people! Either you need to learn to live within your income capabilities, or you learn to work longer or harder. Or, for clever switched-on types, make your investments work smarter!

To remove some of the negative thoughts associated with budgets, I prefer to call your list of 'Income In verses Money Out' a Spending Plan. And, in true learning style, I will repeat this so many times that by the end of the wealth chapter my hope is that you will be compelled to put pen to paper and write your own spending plan!

Use the budget on the following page as a guide.

SPENDING PLAN / BUDGET / LIVING EXPENSES (example)

	Self	Partner	Joint	Total
Tax (if known/self employed)				
Mortgage/Rent				
Loan Repayments / Credit Cards				
Home Maintenance				
Council & Water Rates				
Insurance – Home				
Insurance – Contents				
Insurance – Car & Boat				
Insurance – Personal effects				
Insurance – Life				
Insurance – Income Protection				
Insurance – Other				
Private Health Cover				
Car Registration				
Petrol				
Car Service/Maintenance				
Superannuation				
Regular Savings Plan				
Professional Fees				
Electricity / Gas				
Telephone				
Mobile Phone				
Internet / Pay TV				
Groceries				
Clothing / Shoes				
Education (books/fees)				
Entertainment				
Child Care				
Medical, Dental Expenses				
Pet / Vet care				
Subscriptions & Memberships				
Newspapers/Magazines				
Holidays				
Christmas & Birthdays				
Sports / Hobbies				
Public Transport				
Alcohol & Tobacco				
Hair & Beauty				
Other				
Total Annual Living $				
Add 10% buffer or savings				
Total Annual Living				
Less Annual Income / Wages $				
Surplus / Deficit $				

Expenses

Expenses can be separated into three areas: Fixed Expenses, Non-fixed Expenses and Flexible Expenses.

Fixed Expenses are expenses you cannot change. These expenses occur regularly and cannot be overlooked such as mortgage/rent, school fees, insurance, rates etc. Non-fixed Expenses are expenses that are hard to do without but you may have control on how much you spend by changing your lifestyle and habits, such as food, petrol, telephone bills etc. Finally, there are the Flexible Expenses (sometimes called Discretionary Expenses) which are expenses you would like to have, but can cut down on or even cut out temporarily, if necessary such as magazines, clothes, entertainment, holidays etc.

Split your expenses into these 3 categories. This is a simple way to easily see where you might be able to tighten the reins if you find you have a shortfall.

When you do this exercise, some of you will feel confident it has just reinforced what you already knew – where all the income is going. For others, however, you might feel quite sick and wonder how you are going to change this and create a surplus? Where on earth do you start? Do not despair. Any circumstance can be improved and made to work so you can become financially free. Be committed, follow the plan and get organized.

LIPS Tip 2: Get Financially Organised

Win The Paper Wars – you can't get on top of debt if you don't have a clear idea of where all the paperwork is. A good idea is a large ring binder with dividers. Simple headings like Bank Statements, Credit Card Statements, Insurance, Phone & Power, General Expenses. Place all statements into this folder in date order, keep a box or folder where all receipts go for easy reference. Keep all records for at least five years.

🖋 **Work Out Where You Are At** – It is imperative you follow the Spending Plan to ascertain exactly where your money is coming and going.

🖋 **Cut The Credit** – This applies only if you are in trouble and want to stop yourself getting into deeper debt. If you have more than one credit card, cut the others up. They can be too tempting and are not good for gaining control.

🖋 **Don't apply for more credit** to get out of debt and don't ignore letters from debt collectors. Now is the time to face the music and clear these debts. Contact the people involved, tell them you are working on a budget and plan to pay these debts off. Creditors are more likely to treat you reasonably if you keep them informed; make attempts to make regular payments; show you are making an effort with a budget; do what you say you are going to do; don't let your cheques bounce; and you don't make promises you can't keep. Losing goodwill is not good for your self esteem and confidence with money, nor is it good for your credit rating.

🖋 **Create Direct Debits** – If you have the money to meet payments but miss paying them because you are busy or have lost or misplaced the invoice then ask the company to send a direct debit form. The payments will happen automatically on the due date without you having to think about it. However, if the money is not there you could be hit with a penalty fee.

🖋 **Monthly Check In** – If you can't do it every week, check in with your accounts and bills every month. Make sure they are all filed correctly and all bills are ready to pay on time.

Ways To Make Changes

If you have identified a shortfall in your Spending Plan each month, let me say right from the beginning that I am not here to wield a big whip and lay on the guilt – I am sure some of you will be feeling this already without me adding to it. Effectively your finances are just 'bleeding'. You are spending more than you earn and this will ultimately spell serious trouble. Theoretically all you need to do is stop the bleed, heal the wound and then move on to creating financial freedom for life. This doesn't mean that you must lead a boring, dull and tedious lifestyle for the purposes of saving money to get ahead. Heaven forbid!

Instead, what I want you to understand is that by saving a few dollars here and there you will make terrific headway towards wealth. Some may scoff but believe me, a few dollars saved now will go a very long way towards serious financial wealth – you just need to know how best to use that money which we will talk about later.

You don't always need to show a shortfall to take advantage of the following tips, in fact, those of you who are keen to really get ahead will make investigating ways to save 'moula' a priority!

The place you need to start is in the Flexible Expenses – go through the list, what can you stop, reduce or do without for a while. Be serious here for a minute. Do you seriously want to get off the merry-go-round of financial circles and start to really get ahead? The magazines each week, the regular coffees, lunches and thoughtless additional purchases when you stop to get just milk or fuel. They all add up each week. Do you really need to make all those purchases on your credit cards, the expensive presents, hotel stays, therapies and subscriptions? If you can put these on hold for a while, it won't kill you, and you will be amazed at what a difference it makes at the end of each month.

If you have gone through your Flexible Expenses, now move onto your Non-Fixed Expenses. I am sure there is a few areas in here you can save money as well. Here are a few tried and true suggestions that can help.

LIPS Tips for putting MORE money in your pocket.

🌿 **Food savings** – Don't go shopping if you are hungry! Make a list and stick to it. Buy your fruit and veges at a produce store or better still get them delivered. Shop online, many large supermarket chains now offer this service -you know exactly what you want, you don't get seduced into buying extras and you know exactly how much you have spent. Look at special items. Often home brand items are cheaper and no less in quality. Cook extra at meal times and freeze for nights you don't feel like cooking rather than buying takeaways. Make your lunches. Buy wholesale if you can. Use discount vouchers. Check out Rachael's sensational cookbook she has written with her friend Kim called 4 Ingredients – it saves you a BUCKET of money on groceries.

🌿 **Phone savings** – for family members including teenagers – every time they want to use the phone they have to put 40c in a jar by the phone for the call.

🌿 **Create your spending plan** and add in 10% for savings/emergencies and then stick to it!

🌿 **Reduce the costs on running your car** by having regular tune ups, wheels aligned and tyres inflated. Watch your speed. It can be very expensive, adding to fuel costs, let alone speeding tickets.

🌿 **Pay more off your bad debt** than the minimum required (house, credit card, car loans) – your aim should be to eliminate this type of debt asap.

🌿 **Keep all receipts** in the one place (a box or folder) and if you are really organised keep them in date order. Check them against credit card bills monthly

🌿 **Regularly look over bank statements** including any loan statements to ensure your interest is being charged correctly. Keep an eye on fees and what it costs for electronic and manual transactions.

🦟 If you are going to keep a **credit card** *then aim to pay it* off every month to avoid interest being accrued.

🦟 **Pay your bills and accounts on the last day they are due** to keep the money in your bank or pocket as long as possible. Or set up a direct debit on this date.

🦟 **Kids' Activities** – Make use of cheaper or free attractions. Parks, beaches, gardens, bush walks, pools, museums, libraries and toy libraries.

🦟 **Speak to all your service providers** – home phone, mobile, internet to ensure you are on the correct plan for your needs. Ask your friends who they use and why. Do the same for things like private health insurance, car and house insurance. Shop around and if your provider is not the cheapest see if they will match other quotes before you change.

🦟 *LIPS Tip 3: Make Changes*

Go through all of your expenses/spending and list some ways you would be able to save and make changes quickly and effectively right now.

To save money and live comfortably is achievable. You need to work out what money is going where – then budget in your 'living' money. Don't feel guilty. Your 'living' allocation is just as important in some cases as fuel bills – it makes you happy. Just make sure you budget for it. You can tighten the purse strings (or 'living allowance') when things are a bit of a struggle and then splurge when you have managed to achieve your goals and save for a bit. That is what life is about – give and take.

The biggest, best and most rewarding tip I can give anyone when it comes to spending is :

> Before EVERY purchase, no matter how small, stop and think about whether you really, really need it. Perhaps write this in permanent ink (or sticky note at least) in your wallet when you open it – "Do I really need to buy this?" It will make you stop and think every time!

Get Out Of Debt Strategies

For those of you wanting to get rid of your private debts quickly then I suggest you take a look at one of the following strategies. Discuss with your financial advisor always before undertaking any of them to ensure it is the right strategy for you and your situation.

LIPS Tips for getting out of debt.

Put All Your Debts Into One – Refinancing is a popular strategy. You take a number of different debts and combine them all together, preferably with a low interest rate. The advantage of this is that you only have one repayment to make each month or fortnight and you can save on interest payments.

Pay Higher Interest Debts First – This can give you psychological advantage by paying off some debts faster than the first strategy. It is the sort of strategy that can keep you on track and gives you encouragement as you feel you are getting somewhere.

Pay Smaller Debts Off First – This might not be as good a strategy as the first two as you may end up paying more interest overall. However the feel-good factor as you eliminate some small debts will bring satisfaction and can spur you on to keep going.

Create Creditors Agreements – You might feel sick in the stomach doing this but creditors will certainly appreciate hearing from you, especially if you are willing to make a genuine attempt to pay off the debt. Explain your position and tell them your plan. And whatever you do keep your promises and keep in communication at all times.

Repayment Scheme – This is for serious debt problems and requires a debt repayment scheme approved by the courts. Discuss with your financial advisor to learn more about this strategy.

- **Bankruptcy** – Filing for bankruptcy certainly wipes your debts and gets creditors off your back and although there can be a huge relief in some respects, there are significant potential drawbacks and many negatives you should consider first. This is very serious and needs financial and legal advice.

- **Make More Money** Write down in your journal some ways that you could feasibly create some extra money to add to your household income.

Rather than just looking at ways to reduce spending you could also look at ways to increase your income, (check out Rachael's chapter on creating an income from home on page 165).

Financial Goals

There is no point having a wonderful Spending Plan if you have no idea how to stop the bleeding, with money going out, or know fantastic ways to invest or spend the surplus! People generally don't set goals because of fear of failure, procrastination or not knowing what their goals are. I am sure you have all heard about the power in writing down your goals and reviewing them regularly. Why is it then that many don't do this with money goals? And I don't just mean write the goals of wanting more money. No kidding, everyone wants more money, right?!

You need to get specific with your goals, for example; I want to own my car outright in two years, I want to have no credit card debt in 12 months, I want to have a surplus of $50 per week in my Spending Plan for investment/savings. Your goals need to be clearly defined and believable. Are you really keen to achieve them? Can you truly imagine the benefits?

Let's take someone who wants to save $50 per week towards an investment or savings plan. If they currently spend everything they earn each week how can we achieve this? Go through your Non-Fixed and Flexible Expenses; I am certain you will find areas here where you can save money-a $4 magazine each week, walk if possible instead of taking the car to save on fuel, less junk food in the shopping trolley, reduce takeaway nights, pack your lunch instead of buying it etc. Then, these are all only small changes initially but you can achieve a lot with an extra $50 per week such as reducing your home loan or credit cards significantly therefore reducing the amount of interest payable. Begin a savings plan or investment strategy (such as Dollar Cost Averaging, Installment Gearing etc....more info available on our website for access to this information) or using these available funds to work smarter not harder! This is just a start. Can you imagine what would happen if you really got serious about making money.

There are literally hundreds of ways to get ahead financially and these chapters really only begin to scratch the surface of what is available to you. Just reading and following the exercises is a great start and if you are keen to learn more just refer to our website for more comprehensive seminars, books and articles.

LIPS TIP: What Are Your Financial Goals Take a moment to write down some of your financial goals. Make them specific, give amounts if dollar values are involved. Paint the picture as if it has happened. What do these goals look like if they were true?

What Makes A Good Financial Advisor?

Once you have yourself a budget, especially if you have identified a 'left over amount', you may wish to consider finding a good financial adviser. The best ways to choose your financial planner is as follows: Ask a friend or trusted source (accountant, solicitor) who is happy with their financial adviser) Use the Financial Planning Association's 'Find a Planner' service www.fpa.com.au

Look for someone you can trust. Ideally, someone who you believe is doing well financially (so they are not just all talk, but live the principals themselves!). Be prepared for your meetings and ask lots of questions, no matter how silly they might seem. Do some background checks, internet searches and reading about the firm or planning you are seeing.

Ten good questions to ask a prospective financial planner when you meet them are as follows (as suggested by the Financial Planning Association of Australia):

1. Are you a member of the Financial Planning Association?
2. Are you a Certified Financial Planner™ professional or a practitioner member of the FPA?
3. Can I see your Financial Services Guide?
4. How long have you been a financial planner?
5. What do you specialise in?
6. How do you charge for your services?
7. Will I receive written advice?
8. How often will you review my advice and what will it cost me?
9. If I have any issues with the planner's strategy how will they be resolved?
10. Who authorises you to give advice and are you licensed by ASIC?

The approach to building your wealth is not complicated and nor should it be. The good news is, it's not rocket science and the process can be made simple. In a factual and mathematically researched way, by understanding some basics, it can be very easy to explain – and do.

Great Investment Strategies

> **'The primary goal of investing
> is to derive an income from a source that does not
> involve your personal exertion'**
> Jodie McIver

The approach to building your wealth is not complicated and nor should it be. The good news is, it's not rocket science and the process can be made simple. In a factual and mathematically researched way, by understanding some basics, it can be very easy to explain – and do.

So if becoming wealthy is technically easy, why isn't everyone wealthy? Why is only one out of ten people financially independent? The reason has little to do with circumstance or ability. It's because people either don't budget, they don't have the right information, don't take the time to learn or don't realise they need to. Most people are so caught up in the busy blur of day-to-day life and working for money, they haven't stopped to think about how they might be able to make money work for them.

Before we consider some aspects of wealth creation, and in line with completing the budget we have already talked about, two main areas that are often overlooked are insurances and estate planning.

Insurance

There are two main types of insurance:

- Insuring your possessions (house/contents/motor vehicle)
- Insuring yourself – your life, your income and your health

These days you can protect yourself and your family against a multitude of unforeseen events. I have seen first-hand the negative impacts of no personal insurance and must admit it is a terrible predicament.

Most Australians will adequately insure their possessions. I strongly encourage you see an insurance broker to investigate the options to ensure your property, possessions, business, you and your family are suitably covered. It is traumatic enough to lose a loved one without experiencing financial anguish as well.

Sometimes, depending on your financial situation, the insurance premiums are tax deductible. One such insurance is Income Protection. Insuring your income is very important, especially when investigating the use of debt for any asset purchase. If the debt repayment relies on your personal income then you should seriously consider a form of insurance to protect it.

You should also check your superannuation policies to see if there is an insurance component incorporated. I won't elaborate on the insurance topic except to say that there are many options available in relation to personal insurances and it really is a good idea to see a specialist financial adviser who can tailor the insurances to your situation.

Estate Planning

Estate Planning refers mainly to Wills and Powers of Attorney. A Will is simply a document stating what you want done with your possessions and property after your death. A Will can also nominate guardians for any dependants or children under 18. A Will can also revoke previous wills and you may appoint an Executor who administers your affairs after your death.

Thinking about your death is never a pleasant experience; however I strongly encourage everyone over the age of 18 yrs (or younger if you are a married couple) to make a Will & also consider a Power of Attorney. A Power of Attorney document allows you to give someone you trust the ability to act on your behalf. A document of this nature can be dangerous in the hands of the wrong person. You can outline that the person can only act on your behalf if you are incapacitated by an accident or illness, and only to people you trust to make appropriate decisions.

Equity vs Liability - What You Own Vs What You Owe

One of the key priorities is to get off the merry-go-round of being tied to a labour-based income that is limited by a person's capacity to work (whatever hourly rate they are being paid). The alternative is to build assets that provide income streams so that they are making money regardless of whether you are working. Capital-based income offers far more freedom and flexibility, and the opportunity to be in a far better financial position than is possible through labour-based income. How do we do this? I will explain a bit further.

A big challenge with investing is getting the capital to get started. Firstly, you need to identify the assets you have accrued so far. For the majority of Australians, they have their home in which they live and are paying off a mortgage.

Most people have been brought up with the idea that they need to pay off their home loan. One of the most common phrases I hear is 'I want to own my home'. I completely support the 'theory' of this idea however it really is more a lifestyle choice rather than a business decision. That said, I will always encourage the elimination of the home loan as a priority for most (ie. anything that is not borrowing for investment or income producing purposes). A key note here is the reduction and elimination of any private debt ie. your home loan, credit cards, car loans etc.

Typically, one immediate suggestion in reducing your home mortgage sooner (if you don't have additional investments) is to ensure the loan is 'principal and interest' and make frequent payments either weekly or fortnightly. In addition, try and pay a bit more than your nominated loan repayments per month as this will assist in taking years off your mortgage, you won't necessarily miss the extra money now but you will be very grateful in the future. (Keep an eye on the interest rates charged by your lending institution. Make sure the rate is a competitive one.)

There are other ways to reduce your home loan debt if you have equity and are able to leverage (borrow) against it to invest. I will outline some general ideas further in this chapter. These concepts are not new and can really enhance a person's financial position over time; however are a bit too technical to elaborate on in great detail in these short chapters. With this in mind, I would encourage you to talk to a good financial planner in conjunction with your accountant who will be able to discuss possible scenarios and ideas relating to wealth creation for your individual situation.

Legally Minimize Your Tax

We have all heard the saying, 'there are two things certain in our world – death & taxes'. Paying tax is something we are all familiar with, and without taxes our government imposes we wouldn't have the facilities and services we all use & enjoy daily such as roads, health care & schools. While each Australian will have their own opinion on the subject, our taxation system ensures a certain quality of life and is an ever-changing environment. It is important to note that when you are considering investing, it should always be for 'wealth creation' and not for any perceived tax advantage. Typically, some areas to consider in reducing your taxation, with the help of a specialist tax agent or accountant, is as follows:

🖋 In relation to your occupation, check for all permissible tax deductions: Information for industry specific deductions as well as general deductions are available from the Australian Tax Office (ATO) – visit www.ato.gov.au

🖋 Keep thorough records – While we are on the topic of ATO, you must keep accurate records for a minimum period of 5 years.

🖋 Investment strategies and tax effective investments – borrowing for investment (gearing/leveraging), franked dividends, superannuation etc.

There are numerous taxation benefits with all areas of investment. Consider borrowing to purchase an investment. When you borrow (leverage/gearing) to invest into an asset (shares or property), you can anticipate that for as long as the asset is for investment purposes, then the interest payable on the loan amount is a taxation deduction. So, if you borrowed $100,000 to invest in an asset such as the stock market and your interest rate was 7%, then your total repayments are $7,000 per annum. This $7,000 is a tax deduction to the owner of the investment loan.

Also consider ownership of investments, prepayment,

income splitting and the timing of the income to help minimise taxation. Superannuation may also be an appropriate investment vehicle to choose in order to minimize your taxation and all these concepts can be outlined in detail by a registered tax agent.

Again, it is important to recognize that while you are eligible to receive additional taxation benefits, this should not be your primary reason for undertaking these investments. You should only ever participate in investments for the purposes of creating profit and if you happen to obtain tax benefits along the way then this is a great 'value add' to your wealth creation and should be treated as a bonus.

As with all investments, there is an element of risk. Make sure you ascertain all levels of risk and adopt the 'worst case scenario' for all areas of investing. As with everything, if the decisions you make are based on knowledge, sound advice and having considered the worst case scenario, then you can rest easy and bide your time in periods of market uncertainty or investment downturns.

> *"You miss 100% of the shots you don't take."*
> *Wayne Gretsky*

Creating An Investment Asset Base

As discussed earlier, the primary goal of investing is to derive an income (and/or capital growth depending on how you view it) from a source that does not involve your personal exertion. One way to make this possible is by having your capital base working for you.

Borrowing To Invest

Investing successfully is all about fulfilling your full financial potential, not about being constrained by the limits of your present position, no matter how big those limits may be! Recent surveys reveal that almost half of the Australian population is unable to allocate any of their income to their bank account for savings. More tragically, there is not enough money in their income to spend at their discretion. Most people find there is always a shortfall of income to do the things they are passionate about. This can be very limiting.

When someone borrows in order to invest, this is known as *leveraging* or *gearing* into the investment. This approach allows the returns from the investment (dollar value) to be much higher than could be achieved using an investor's own money (without gearing) mainly because of the increased size of the capital base (that is borrowed and invested). This method of increasing the dollar value of returns by borrowing means that (in percentage terms) the return on your *own* dollars invested has outperformed what the market has delivered.

Borrowing to invest is not a new concept and can magnify any asset returns, but it is very important to note that while *gearing* increases investment returns above the market average in a rising market, *there is also a magnification of negative returns* in a falling market. In a downward trending market, the loss in the value of the dollar is greater with geared investments, so in percentage terms, losses will be greater than that experienced by the market overall.

When referring to the share market, and give this market rises on average more than it falls (and so the trend is upwards), you can anticipate that the positive outcomes achieved from gearing in a rising market will outweigh the negative outcomes of gearing in a falling market. Over the medium to longer term, the net (after tax) effects of gearing will be to add value to your investments. It is always important to note however that the stock market experiences inevitable downturns and your own emotional state needs to also be brought into the equation.

Another important part of this whole scenario of becoming a capitalist (using geared investing) is the appropriate level of cash reserves available in the portfolio to act as a buffer against market volatility in the short term. Adequate cash reserves ensure liquidity and acts as a safety net in the event of unforeseen circumstances. Having cash reserves also ensures you can take advantage of market fluctuations and volatility.

Only consider borrowing if you are going to invest the funds into good quality assets and not for private or consumption purposes (not the latest plasma screen for the lounge room!). As long as you take a logical, knowledgeable view - allow sufficient time, cash reserves, and invest in quality assets - geared investments can be an ideal tool for wealth creation. You can then think about using profits from your investments to pay cash for life's luxuries instead of always putting them on credit cards or personal loans.

Investors should think seriously about gearing if you have a long-term outlook towards investment, and the need or desire to accumulate wealth more quickly than you can by using only your own funds to invest. It is important to note the minimum time that you should contemplate for a geared investment into shares is 7 to 10 years. Property investment needs an even longer timeframe – preferably 15 years. Even though gearing has great potential tax advantages it is of secondary importance. The ability gearing can give you to own a larger, and perhaps better quality portfolio than you could otherwise afford is crucially important. Never gear (borrow) purely for tax advantages.

Another important part of your planning process, especially if you rely on a continual income stream from work to pay the interest on borrowed funds, is protecting yourself with insurance. Be cautious and conservative when borrowing against assets such as your home because if you default on the loan it could mean the loss of your house. This is why I strongly suggest speaking with a specialist financial planner about the above concepts, safety parameters and appropriate borrowing levels to ensure you are purchasing quality investment assets with your borrowed funds and have plenty of cash reserves.

Where To Invest?

Now that we understand the importance of borrowing to invest (not borrowing for plasma screens!). Where do we put these funds? Typically, there are only three places you can invest your funds:

- Cash
- Property
- Shares.

The herd mentality suggests that shares are the most risky, then property and the least risky is cash. History shows that shares will outperform property, and property will outperform cash over the longer term. So, if we understand that shares are going to perform better over time, which shares do you invest in? My thoughts are that rather than picking or choosing individual shares or fund managers to make the decisions for you, a good approach is to invest in all of the shares in the top 300 on the Australian Stock market…via an Index Fund.

What Is Indexing?

Indexing is an investment strategy that attempts to match closely the investment returns of a specific group of shares, bonds or other securities, usually represented by a recognized benchmark such as the ASX All Ordinaries Index.

The Investment manager constructs a portfolio which closely tracks this benchmark by holding all, or a representative sample, of the securities in the index. Investors pay traditional "active" investment managers to take their 'bets' on individual shares or industry sectors to try to outperform the benchmark.

Investors in index funds accept investment returns which match the performance of the benchmark in return for lower management fees.

'The Australian Financial Review' Jan 31-Feb 1 1998

Annual movement of Australian shares

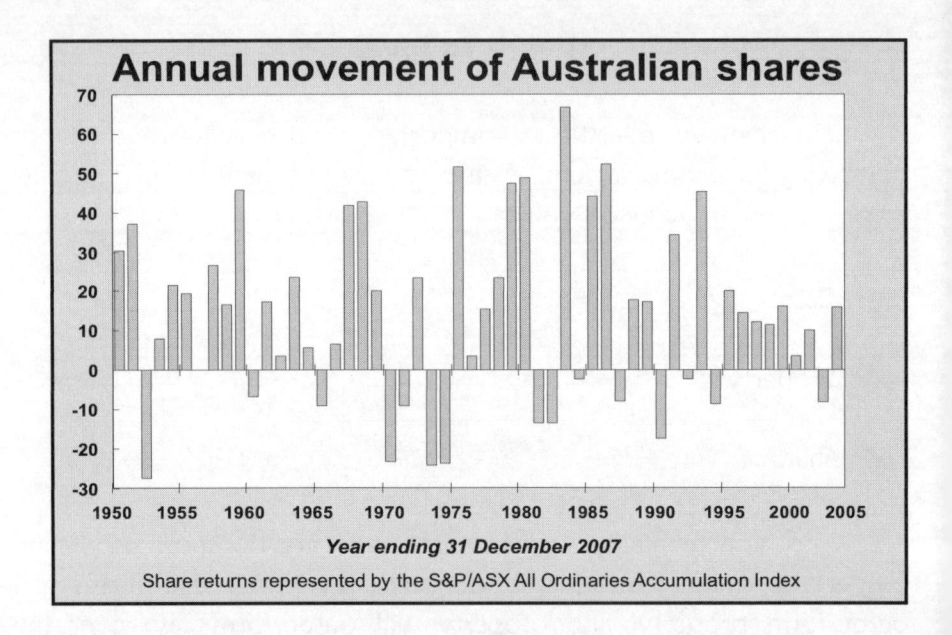

Year ending 31 December 2007

Share returns represented by the S&P/ASX All Ordinaries Accumulation Index

You can see by this chart that there are more 'positive' years than 'negative years'. Creating an investment portfolio that closely tracks the All Ordinaries Index and holding this investment over time may enhance your overall wealth creation. To embrace the volatility (highs and lows), you need to take advantage of market lows -that is have sufficient cash reserves and unused equity to invest when the market is trending downwards. Then, when the markets are in 'good years' and trending upwards you may consider taking profits to either pay out private debt or add to your cash reserves for income.

Managing any stock market volatility through the markets is technically easier to understand but emotionally harder to do. By ignoring speculative and short-term investing, you need to view the volatility of the stock market as a huge advantage as explained above. Then, work out a good system (or have a planner put one in place) that manages and monitors your investments through the market's movements. By doing this, you effectively allow the long-term and exponential growth to emerge.

Retirement strategies

Even though we have specifically outlined a wealth creation type strategy, there are numerous ways to maximize your retirement income if you have already embarked (or are close to) on this journey. Again, good financial advice is essentially to ensure you have maximised your investment returns, minimised any taxation payable and incorporated a high level of safety to your strategy.

Summary

Education is the key element in any successful endeavour. These short chapters have only just scratched the surface and the suggestions made here are only a few from potentially thousands of investment options you can investigate. Again, the information outlined in these short chapters is for general information only and is not specific to your individual needs. With this in mind, it should not be acted upon without prior reference to your particular circumstance, needs and objectives, current economic conditions and financial adviser's advice (or investment specialist).

Don't expect to learn & understand all of this overnight; remember anything worthwhile takes time. Ask questions, challenge people to give you answers and then make up your own mind on what is best for you. Engage the use of professionals (financial advisers, accountants etc) you can really talk to. What drives them? Are they always acting in your best interest? At the end of the day, it is your life...you really need to make the most of it! Surround yourself with people who will encourage your potential to be amazing.

No doubt you are working really hard now to earn a decent living and you have given thought to how you want to grow your personal wealth. Expect any changes to begin with you. A good attitude to adopt is that you are striving to become a capitalist....someone who earns income from assets, rather than from personal exertion. Remember, the amount of capital you have, or can amass, with conventional savings and investment programs are unlikely to be sufficient for your retirement – so explore all the options. Good fortune is something you can create!

I hope I have inspired you a little to go and investigate your own financial situation further. The most important thing is that you start the process. I sincerely urge you to give high priority to seeking good financial advice and all the rewards such guidance bring. Then, the way you need to measure your success is….*will you ultimately have the funds you need to be free to enjoy life and do whatever it is you want to do?*

> *Our deepest fear is not that we are inadequate. Our deepest fear is that we are powerful beyond measure. It is our light, not our darkness, that most frightens us. We ask ourselves, who am I to be brilliant, gorgeous, talented and fabulous? Actually, who are you not to be?"*
> Nelson Mandela

Creating An Income From Home

> *'From every adversity lays a great opportunity for growth'*
> Rachael Bermingham

Five years ago, I decided I wanted to have children but I still wanted to remain active within business and receive an income; the logical choice for me was to think about building a business from home. It took months of planning and some *really* long hours to get my first business up and running to a profitable stage but it's something I am so happy I have done. It's absolutely BRILLIANT to be able to set your own work hours, work around your family commitments and still create and receive a healthy income – for me it's *everything* I wanted and more but it took lots of work and still does.

However once you know the process – it's relatively straight forward and you can duplicate the process for multiple businesses. Now, five years later, I solo run and co-manage a number of businesses that provide my family with a fabulous income. The input I have into each business is taken during my sons sleep time which means *most* days I live a happy balance of being the hands on, loving, and attentive Mum I always aspired to be, as well as being a great friend and wife AND a successful business woman. To do this as well as still fit in the additional activities of having a TV Show (4 Ingredients on the LifeStyle Channel), numerous interviews, writing books and managing 3 businesses does take takes a little juggling, however with proper planning, everything usually goes smoothly and life, although fast paced, is mostly pretty relaxed. I'm often asked to share my story, so at the insistence of the other authors on these following pages I'll do just that in the hope that if creating an income does interest you, then it may also inspire you to achieve your professional success on your own terms too.

After a host of fun vocations such as hairdressing and shark diver/feeder at Underwater World, my real and more serious professional interest and success was born seven years ago when I opened a travel agency 3 months prior to September 11 and consequently lost everything I owned. I didn't know it at the time, but it would prove to change my career for the BEST! The travel trade went into a downward spin and it only got worse from there with Ansett and Canada 300 collapsing, then the horrific Bali Bombings, the outbreak of the SARS virus and Iraqi War all of which contributed to crippling my infant travel agency. They say that from every adversity lays a great opportunity for growth and this proved very true in my circumstance.

With debt up to my eyeballs from a series of long leases on computer systems, printers, safes, phone systems and of course retail rental space, a team of four *and* no income coming in (people were too scared to get on a bus let alone a plane!) I simply didn't have anything to spend on advertising my business. I had heard the old saying that marketing is the oxygen of all successful businesses, and is *also* 80% of the business, so I thought I had better start learning how to market, NOW!!

After taking a good look at my business I was stunned to find that more than 70% of customers were either repeat or had been referred and the thousands of dollars I had been spending accounted for a *tiny* 1% of my business! With this in mind I knew that my customer service was brilliant but my client numbers (being a new agency) where still far too low to make the business profitable. I HAD to learn other ways to get customers in the door and survive the travel industries most ruinous era.

I researched and tested LOTS & LOTS (and *LOTS!*) of strategies and eventually learned the art of marketing and publicity, and to my surprise I found I LOVED it *and thankfully* had a real knack for it. *Fortunately* my talent soon became quite a talking point and I began to receive requests to help others. My passion for travel waned and my desire to start a family increased along with my interest in marketing. So a plan was put into place to wind up the agency and start my marketing consultancy business from home. I took on my first marketing client and to the absolute delight of the two women who owned the business, the marketing strategy I designed and implemented worked and they went from a tiny turnover to a $2.5 million turnover within five months.

I soon built my business up and went onto mentor and consult women in six different countries on how to build their own businesses through marketing, publicity and other business strategies like planning. Now it may look like it was a walk in the park, but I can tell you it definitely wasn't. It took a lot of courage to do it especially since I had a MASSIVE debt from the agency in leases etc to the tune of well over $300,000. My VERY supportive husband and I lived on his wage of just over $500 a week while I worked my tush off to get the business going against the advice of our solicitor who at the time said 'For goodness sake Paul and Rachael – go bankrupt it's *too* huge a debt to carry and it'll take you a lifetime to pay it off'. Even though I'm glad we didn't take his advice, there were days and days and *days* when I was worn down to the quick from the daily ritual of answering the phone and telling creditors that I WOULD pay my debt to them but to *please* be patient with me!!

The motivation to make money was a very, very high priority!! Bankruptcy for us just wasn't an option, I didn't feel comfortable knowing there were people out there who I owed money to, so with the support, patience and encouragement of Paul, we decided to basically work our backsides off and plough every cent we earned into the debt which we eventually paid off within 4 years.

It took 6 months for me to regain my professional confidence again and start to see the worldly happenings as a gift without which I would never have learnt how to market *without* spending a cent, play *without* a cent, and budget with very little cents! I am thankful my experience also gives others hope when they *feel* like they are failing, there's *always* a positive in EVERY situation.

I have since gone on to co write 3 books with a 4th and 5th on the way along with building my speaking business (I speak at seminars on life balance, time management, goal achievement, planning for success, marketing and how to build a business from home successfully) and Sunshine Coast Speakers Bureau which I manage with Cyndi. The marketing I learnt during my travel days has been the key ingredient to the success in this book you are reading, my other co authored books and each of my businesses as well as those of others I have consulted to over the years.

Business is a passion of mine. Today, you can do business in a number of ways, from a shop front to leasing space in someone else's office, being out on the road, doing tradeshows, or, my personal favourite; from your home office, lounge room, kitchen table or even poolside in your own backyard! I've done business just about everywhere (within reason!)

This flexibility makes it highly attractive and possible for almost anyone to start a business, but with around 75% of businesses failing in the first five years, it is imperative you go into it from a 'business' perspective rather than a 'hobby' perspective. It's absolutely fantastic to make a career out of doing what you love, but it can get stressful and wearing if you're not earning a wage and making a profit from it.

I'll tell you straight up that from my experience – you'll need *lots* of energy, time, passion and planning before you even start, but I can honestly say it is sooooooooooo worth it! So many people have lost partners and precious moments with family and friends, not to mention enduring decreased quality of and life and health. Women are an amazing, wonderful, skillful, intelligent and multi-faceted breed. We can do a multitude of things at any given time successfully; however, but we do have a tendency to do too much (way too much at times!), which is where we can come unstuck in business.

To create an income from home, there are some qualities you need to have in place before you begin your journey into the business world.

The first one is often overlooked due to the lure of the dollar. It's **PASSION!** Whatever you do, you *must* be passionate about it. Customers *love* the energy and atmosphere of passionate people! Just as negativity in the workplace spreads like a disease, so too does passion *but* with a far better, healthier and happier purpose. If you love what you do, your enthusiasm, positivity, energy and excitement will serve to inspire, attract and *engage* your customers. Instead of having to 'sell yourself', you'll only need to 'educate your customer' about your product, service or information.

Passion conveyed is an integral ingredient to prospering in business and the best way to gauge your passion is to ask yourself whether you would still do this even if you didn't earn a single dollar from it. Are you *so* passionate that *you can't wait* to jump out of bed and get into your business day? If you aren't excited about what you do, then it's quite possible that you have customers, work mates, family and friends who wish you would change careers too! So get passionate! After all, if *you're* not happy about what you do, why on earth would your customers be happy to do business with you?

If you would like to start your own business and don't know what your passion is, try this little exercise that I've done when I've needed some direction in the past.

Make a list of the following:

- Things you love

- Activities you love doing

- Talents and skills you have

- The most frequent qualities about yourself that you get complimented on and the things you can do with ease

- Careers, activities you would like to do

- Things you have an interest in or are drawn to

- Information or knowledge you've acquired over the years that could benefit lots of other people

From this list, pluck out the ones you could potentially create an income from, or *those that could contribute to creating an income in a joint venture partnership with someone with a complementary skill.* This will give you more clarity and direction for possible income potential that you can explore.

Most people think business is about their product, but it's not. The product is only the vehicle. The real secret to business success is **ADDING VALUE**. The best question to ask yourself before you even start to build a foundation for your business is, how can you add value to your customers? What sort of value can you provide that will help make their lives easier, more enjoyable, less stressful and more fulfilled. Think of yourself as a problem solver. What *problem* are you solving for people? It doesn't matter what business you are in – if you're in business we have one thing in common and this is we are all problem solvers.

It's amazing what happens when you think in these terms. Spend a moment considering it now. You have a car to solve the problem of getting from one place to another, a fridge to solve the problem of your food going off, a phone to solve the problem of not being able to talk to someone right away, a TV to solve the problem of being bored etc. So what problem are you going to be solving for someone else? Furthermore (thinking even bigger now), what else can you do to add even more value to their lives while solving that problem? What problem may they encounter in the near future that you can create a vehicle (product or service) for, to help them solve that problem as well? Mmmmm the imagination is running wild (at least I hope it is!).

So this is really where you need to start thinking from once you have uncovered what you're passionate about. Grab a pen and paper and start writing out ways your passion can add value to lots of people by solving a problem that they have right now or in the future?

The next ingredient in achieving prosperity is **PLANNING**. What are the chances of you climbing into the cockpit of an airplane and flying it without prior instruction? I'd be guessing (but almost certain) that it would be Buckley's and none, yes? So if you've never been in business before, would it be wise to attempt it without prior instruction, research or planning? No of course not. Now I can say (and with great conviction) that after 20 years of business experience, I truly didn't know the real value of basic leg work, planning and research until much later in my business life.

There is a saying that goes, 'If you fail to plan, you plan to fail', *and* if you don't have a plan or map of where you are going, then how do you know where you'll end up? It all sounds a little tedious – all this research and planning – doesn't it? I thought so earlier on in business and as a result I paid the price with more than just a few crash landings! Being a headstrong, adventurous, over-excited and impatient woman can certainly have its good points and it can also be problematic as well, particularly if you don't slow down long enough to plan sufficiently. Take it from me, not only have I flown the plane without instruction, I've also jumped out of it WITHOUT a parachute more times than I'd like to admit!

I know I'm making light of this, but I can tell you I bore more weight in stress, financial pressure and wasted time and energy than was ever necessary. Had I taken some time to plan properly, be clear on what value (and potential value) I add, checked if the idea was worth my while by doing a SWOT analysis (Strengths, Weaknesses, Opportunities, Threats), got some ongoing financial instruction and checkups on my cash flow and budget, as well as learning how to look after my profits, I could have saved myself hundreds of thousands of dollars and fast-tracked to achieve my goals many years ago.

UNDERSTAND WHAT YOU ARE GOOD AT and outsource or find other people to do the rest! It's no fun at all doing something that you don't enjoy. I used to procrastinate so long on doing things like entering data into my accounts system, that by the time I did it, the task was so overwhelming it took forever to do, and by that time I was one unhappy, stressed and time-challenged woman. The time I wasted on thinking about having to do it, added to the fact that I didn't do it well anyway, ended up costing much more than if I had outsourced the job in the first place. Now, I know my place (so to speak) and have happily handed the task over to a fabulous lady who just *loves* doing it. She is great at it because she's passionate about it.

Whoever said 'know your weaknesses and work on them' was crazy! I'm so much happier since I delegated the things I don't like doing; it actually frees me up to work in areas that are more income-producing so I can achieve my goals. *Plus*, it's easier, cheaper, and heaps more fun! When the **LIPS** (Ladies Initiating Prosperity & Success) concept was born, I sought out the people who were as passionate about their interests as I am about mine. The result is that we have every area covered incredibly well as we each enjoy what we do. It works superbly. No one does anything they don't like doing or aren't good at, so it's a win for all of us and a win for people dealing with us.

Anyone starting a business needs to **DREAM BIG**. Your success can only be as big as your dreams and the more you stretch yourself, the more you'll be surprised at how far you can go. Just take a moment and look around the room that you're sitting in right now. Every single thing you can see was once someone's dream. Take little steps and put in the time, creativity and energy to nurture your dream.

GET ORGANISED so you can ensure you have the time to develop your passion. Being in business can be challenging at times, and when you couple that task with being a mum, it becomes even trickier. You need to be focused, passionate, driven, energetic, creative and strategic, as well as being sales person, marketer, accountant, administrator, trouble shooter, techie, cleaner, secretary, teacher, counselor, confidante and gofer – and that's all before you knock off for the day to be Mum, wife and friend!

So if you're a mum, you'll need to rely on a strict schedule to ensure you don't burn out, otherwise something will give (and the first three to go are usually your health, your relationship with your partner, and the business you've been building). If you get through your days feeling somewhat pressured, chaotic and stressed, and crawl into bed and take what feels like your first breath for the day, then you know you need help to maximize your time more efficiently *(see the Life Balance chapter)*.

Seek out various **mentors** who have 'been there, done that', not only do you often save thousands of dollars, but you can achieve the success you desire a lot more quickly.

Successful, high-profile people such as Oprah, Tiger Woods and Madonna have known the real value of having coaches and mentors for many, many years (and mind you, were really the only ones who could afford them too!). However, in the past few years, having a mentor or two has become accessible and affordable to almost everyone. Having mentors is a wonderful way to keep on track, brainstorm and talk business when everyone else is sick to death of hearing about it! I've had numerous mentors along the way, each one as valuable as the next, and this has helped me evolve and achieve my business goals.

BIG PICTURE – What do you want this business to do and be? How long do you see yourself having it? Do you plan to sell it in the future or do you plan to hand it down to family or a loyal employee?

These bigger-picture questions will help you define a clear picture of the purpose of your business, and this is important because it will help you make more focused business decisions along the way. Too many proprietors spend (waste) thousands of dollars, due to not knowing what their plan for the business is.

Other questions about your role in the business are just as important, such as:

- Where do you see yourself this time next year?

- What goals do you wish to accomplish within the business?

- How much time do you intend to work 'in' your business (doing the do)?

- How much time do you intend to work 'on' your business (being strategic and planning how to build/develop it)?

- How much time do you intend to have 'out' of your business (play time away from your business with family and friends for R&R, space to clear your head and recharge your batteries)?

If you take the time to even think about these things, you'll not only be one step ahead of many others, but you'll also start to see what it's going to take from you to make it happen, *and* if it's what you really want. Bump some of these things around with a supportive (but honest) friend to ensure you are getting into business for the right reasons; after all – you DO want to be profitable.

WATCH YOUR PENNIES! Value the dollars you earn and don't be extravagant (I learnt this the hard way). Whatever you pay out, ask yourself if it directly or indirectly will be instrumental in you achieving your goal and could you still achieve the outcome without it for now. A new computer, for instance, may not be necessary; you can do most things quite easily without a flashy, new computer. Be realistic. I'd rather see those profits remaining in your account than being paid out for things that are not really necessary, leaving you short on cash flow and stressed-out, wouldn't you?

BE YOURSELF -Hone in and develop your own personal brand, step into your authentic self and enjoy the ride! Confidence comes from being comfortable in your own skin. It's a lovely way to live and everyone, including your customers, will be happier when you're happy.

You've probably heard the quote 'If you build it they will come' (from the movie *Field of Dreams*), and yes, they probably WILL come, but how many and how quickly will depend on your **MARKETING** (for more information go to my website www.RachaelBermingham.com). While the seeds for success in business are dreaming, passion and belief, and the nutrients are planning and research, the oxygen for any business is definitely marketing.

Small business is a major part of our economy and you can join in on the action too in a variety of ways. If you haven't already got a business you love or don't have any ideas springing to mind, take a look at these ideas and you may just be inspired by one or two.

LIPS Tips for creating an income from home;

If you have a spare room, take in a student or boarder into

your home – I did this for a year and it was not only culturally educational it was also financially helpful as well.

🌱 Use your knowledge – people are time poor these days so if they can fast track with a one on one session with another to help them on a topic then THIS is a smart way to succeed. Don't be afraid to share your knowledge for a profitable purpose.

🌱 Sell someone elses product that you love. When the movie The Secret first came out I created a website, marketed it and sold it through this avenue. I've believed in this philosophy for more than 20 years, so becoming an affiliate for a product such as this one was easy.

🌱 If you have administration ability – become a 'virtual' personal assistant – this is basically a PA who works from their home office. I have a gorgeous Mum who is my virtual assistant.

🌱 If you LOVE figures or data entry – why not become a bookkeeper, the going rate is now $45 per hour minimum which based on 10 hours a week will give you a nifty $450 in your pocket.

🌱 Love words? Proofreading, editing and typesetting is big business these days too.

🌱 If you love having a chat, then try your hand (or should I say ear) at being an over the phone mystery shopper or if you love shopping then maybe an in-store mystery shopper?

🌱 If you have a curious nature then maybe researching is more your cup of tea.

🌱 If you have a product to sell and don't have a website, then check out my www.RachaelBermingham.com site – this is a website that has cost me all up $120 and that included 1 year of hosting. It's basic but all I need to share the information about my speaking. If you want to make extra income you can also sign up for Google ads and receive an income this way too.

🌿 If you're creative behind the camera - try photography. Wedding and family photography is always a fabulous income source.

🌿 Maybe you're handy with a sewing machine and can take some beautiful clothes for an income?

🌿 Gardening, landscaping designing.

🌿 Graphic Artistry.

🌿 Lessons on just about anything! Guitar, piano, singing (if you're in the Sunny Coast area let me know and I'll employ you to help me sing so I don't give my family and more grief with my divine singing!), swimming, running, basketball, beauty, health, business the list is literally endless!

LIPS Tips for Teenagers to create an income from home

🌿 Cleaning

🌿 Filing

🌿 Data entry

🌿 Sell old CD's, old technology, games, clothes on Ebay

🌿 Hunt through second hand stores for groovy (or is that sick – what word is 'cool' these days?) clothes and sell them

- Car washing.

- Tutoring.

- Direct Selling. There are numerous sensational direct selling businesses out there that you can develop and manage in your own time and there's a lot of money to make within them. This option is fabulous if you don't like to run solo. You always have someone to call upon to ask questions and usually there is a system they give you on how to develop your business and how to make it profitable. Like all businesses – success always depends on the effort you put in to it. Usually there is a buy in figure that you will need to pay up front, this is mostly for the support and continued guidance they give to you and some product as well. I've met some incredibly happy and wealthy people revelling in a variety of direct selling businesses so if you'd like to check out more information about this type of business go to our website www.ReadMyLips.com, you will find a link there to a site that lists all of them.

*Remember – if you don't have a go –
you'll never know what you're missing…*

To sum it up,

> PASSION + PLANNING + PERSISTANCE +
> PATIENCE + POSITIVITY + PROACTIVITY =
> PROFIT

Remember what we said in the beginning,

Every single success you have ever achieved required action and implementation. To change your world you first need to change yourself and this is not for the fainthearted. But know this: if you weren't up to the task then this book would never have found you. So be brave, be strong, love and value yourself.

Keep yourself focused on positivity with the following LIPS Manifesto, and get out there be proud of who you really are and live the life you've always desired.

The Lips Manifesto

For A Healthy, Wealthy, Vibrant And Passionate Life!

Here is something that could literally change your life and help you to live the life you have always dreamed of living. Consciously say (in other words really think about this Manifesto as you say it) – you could even use this one as a template and create your own (as mentioned in the Conscious Creation chapter).

Implement the Manifesto on a daily basis and you will most certainly create and attract the magic you deserve.

'I (your name) .....' (or you can also affirm by saying) 'I....'

- Will remember health is my greatest asset. I always invest time, energy and a never-ending commitment to it - for life.

- Will drink at least eight glasses of pure water every day.

- LOVE getting my body moving! I exercise with excitement and do something every day – even if it is only 10 sit-ups or 10 press-ups on a busy day! I know that regular exercise coupled with high quality nutrition is the key to longevity and wellbeing.

- Enjoy giving myself a daily body massage using pure essential oils.

- Know by concentrating and focusing on the great things I do have, I will receive of lot more of them into my life.

- Understand now that by being grateful, I will feel better about myself and others.

- Feel great pleasure when I admire and take in the beauty of nature, giving thanks for it and respecting it allow others to enjoy its beauty also.

- Remember each morning to take a natural antioxidant and mineral supplement daily to assist in helping me keep at the top of my health and wellbeing game.

- Benefit greatly from getting back to the most natural source when feeding my body; the less processed a food, the more nutrients I know I will fuel my body with.

- Feed my skin with vital ingredients from Mother Nature's kitchen. I only choose products that truly represent Natural.

- Read an inspirational book at least once a month.

- Enjoy getting up early to experience the freshness of a new day.

- Keep clutter to a minimum.

- Am grateful for my body whatever shape or size.

- Bring nature indoors with Aromatherapy and light my vaporiser and fill it with water and pure essential oils every day.

- Bring the beauty of fresh flowers indoors – even if it is only a daisy.

- Know going to sleep on an argument will not only decrease my quantity of sleep it will also decrease my quality of sleep. I ensure I go to bed with peace each night.

- Use travelling time as a chance to hear music, an audio or sing out loud.

- Acknowledge we have unique and sometimes challenging personality traits. I accept we are different but not wrong and will try to speak into others needs not just my own.

- Give myself some quiet time everyday – even if it is 5 minutes in the toilet!

- Read a quote, a poem or a story that inspires me every day.

- Keep a journal of my thoughts, dreams, visions and experiences so I can remember to celebrate who I am and my successes.

- Smile when I answer the phone.

- Treat others as I would like to be treated myself.

- Believe I can do anything so others will too.

- See a challenge as a chance to grow.

- Will always put my personal relationships, loved ones and family first ALWAYS!

- Will have the courage to look to others for support and advice and be there for others in return.

- Love sharing my goals and dreams so they may take shape and actually occur.

- Read food labels and become aware of what they mean before casually placing food and skin care items in my trolley.

- Delight in eating fresh fruit and vegetables daily and choose organic where I can.

- Recycle whenever possible.

- Graze not gorge! Eating 5-6 regular meals a day to keep my metabolism and energy up.

- Have regular body work at least once a month. I see this as a necessity (not a luxury) for me in creating a healthy legacy for my children and family.

- Keep a natural First Aid Kit stocked with remedies like Arnica, Rescue Remedy, Tea Tree, Lavender and Calendula Cream.

- Treat money with respect and welcome wealth and abundance into my life.

- Respect my peers and honour the work other people do.

- Am kind to myself – understanding while over indulging has its consequences that there is such a things as the 80:20 rule so I will nurture and honour my body back to health when I wake!

- Learn from our children. Look at life with their simplicity and their ability to live in the present and acknowledge all people and things with acceptance.

- Learn from my elders. It is from them I can gain great wisdom.

- It makes my spirit sour when I laugh out loud – and I know this is the best medicine of all.

- Am thrilled at understand that my body is a highly intelligent entity and can fix and heal itself a lot of the time if I give it the opportunity to do so.

- Fill my head with positive thoughts because I know it helps me to achieve my goals.

- Will speak my truth and walk my talk – because I understand that by doing this – my head, heart and actions are congruent and all moving in the same direction.

- Will keep my mind open to new opportunities and let the universe/god guide me to experiencing new things that will assist me to grow in terms of health, wealth, life and spirit.

- Celebrate life with passion!

BEAUTIFUL LIPS WOMEN

When a little girl is 3, she looks at herself and sees a glorious Queen
Her world is like all the fairytale books she's ever read and seen
By the time she reaches 8, she sees herself as Sleeping Beauty
She plays the part she is a princess, the sweetest little cutie.

But when she hits her teens its like she sees nothing nice at all
All she sees are ugly pimples, too fat, too short, too tall
This crazy self-destruction continues into her 20's andbeyond
Perfect images make her wish for a magic modelmaking wand.

And then she hits her 30's, life's busy now with so much to do
She's fatter now but what the heck, she's had a kid or two
She feels herself getting older, she complains and knows its naughty
She's got more wrinkles, a mid life crisis, and she's hitting 40!

She tries real hard to say 'I'm ok' but the mirror doesn't lie
She's put on weight, tried all the diets, its enough to ake her cry
What she'd give to have her body of twenty years ago
If only she'd had more time for her, she'd have made an effort you know!

Then something starts to happen at 50, a woman takes heed and reflects within
She looks at herself, she says 'I am', she will conquer, prevail and win
She tells young women be kind to yourself, be happy with who you are
When youth passes you by you will reflect
and see you were indeed a shining star.

A 60 year old woman looks at herself and is grateful she can see at all
She reminds herself how short life is, there's no too fat, too tall
She sees all women as beautiful if only they weren't in such a hurry
She says slow down smell the roses, stop all the fuss and worry.

When a woman is 70 she looks at herself and sees the wisdom and laughter
Life is about enjoying yourself being loved and happy ever after
Having a body that moves with ease, an active and open mind
Knowing that beauty lies within, being truthful, honest and kind.

An 80- year old woman doesn't look at herself, she sees the wind, the rain, the sun
She puts on a pink hat goes out in the world and shares it with everyone
If only we knew to grab that pink hat and see the world through her eyes
Judge ourselves less and learn to appreciate that life is the greatest prize.

There is no reason why we shouldn't all smile and see how beautiful we are
Women take stock, accept who you are, be the light in your shining star
Honour yourself, love who you are and develop your own new creed
Take time out, indulge yourself, it's the LIPS woman's way indeed!

Kim Morrison © 2008

Author's Acknowledgements

From Rachael

To my ever-loving, supportive, patient and *very* beautiful husband Paul, thank you for ALWAYS being there, believing in me, and being as passionate about my dreams as I am. I admire you and love you for being the amazing person you are. To my gorgeous 3 year old son Jaxson, for your endless smiles and being the best boy ever at our *numerous* meetings. You're already a STAR and I love you more than I could have ever imagined. You are my inspiration to *be* better and *do* better every day, and to create a legacy that will enable you to be all that you wish to be too.

To the best friend a girl could ever ask for – Boof; I am forever grateful our paths crossed. Our every encounter is SO much fun, I am fortunate to have a best friend like you! Spud and Debbie for always showing a genuine interest in me, and my family. To Dad for your love and patience. To Mum for showing me how to be independent. To Lee and Terri for the adventures – never a dull moment thankfully!

To my business partner & friend Cyndi O'Meara for helping me to develop a healthy legacy for my family which is invaluable. My life-long friend and 4 Ingredients partner Kim McCosker a gorgeous lady who has taught me so many things in our 37 years of being friends, it would literally be a book in itself! Thank you ladies for giving me the professional space I need in order to fill my creative cup. To the Kellys for always being amazing friends. To Kimmy Morrison for all your support and help whenever I've needed it –thanks babe!

To the LIPS girls collectively, without you, this would all still be a dream. Thank you for your energy, enthusiasm, time and love. And finally to every courageous, funny, honest, strong, and dedicated woman who continues to do their very best each and every day please remember your smile, kind words, winks and shows of affection both big and small are incredibly inspirational and helpful to others every day – keep sharing these simple things to contribute in building happier, healthier and wealthier, more loving and peaceful communities.

From Cyndi

I am the person I am today at age 48 because of the people I've met and the things that have happened to me, so I'd like to acknowledge those I've encountered for a brief moment, those who have been around for a long time, and others in between – so many have helped shape the path of my life.

Of course my parents Janet and David and siblings Lisa and Marcus have been very influential – especially my sister who is so wise and full of knowledge and always seems to know the answer to the many questions I throw at her.

I have many friends I cannot name in this small space – you know who you are. Special thanks go to two very special friends who are always there for me, Rikki Latcham and Anna Kurz Rogers, and of course to my very special **LIPS** friends, Rachael Bermingham, Kim Morrison, Fleur Whelligan, Jodie McIver and Allie Mooney.

My husband Howard and my children, Fran, Brogan, Casie and Tarnea are my greatest teachers and joy and the ones I really want to thank. Thank you for the love, honesty, encouragement, teachings, fun, tears and laughter in my life. I also thank you for – Reason. Without a reason for doing things, nothing seems worthwhile. I love you all.

From Kim & Fleur

We acknowledge the extraordinary Rachael Bermingham for initiating this project and inviting us to be part of it. And to the other gorgeous authors Cyndi, Allie, Jodie and Michelle who bring gifts that are truly inspirational, we thank you all.

We often leave acknowledging our husbands until the end but this time, Dave and Danny, we salute you at the beginning. In the fifties, women were encouraged to prepare the home, the children and the meal, have lipstick on, look gorgeous and be ready and waiting for their husband to arrive home from a long day at work. We know some days you would like to be transported back in time! However, you have to put up with two unstoppable, Aries women who are always on a mission! Often you have to step in and put the apron on yourselves. We want to thank you both for all that you do. You know we could never do it without you. We are incredibly blessed to be sharing our lives and dreams together. You are divine husbands and wonderful fathers and we love you to bits!

We have been inspired by many different, multitasking, dynamic and beautiful women we have met throughout our lives. It is hard to acknowledge everyone here, but we do thank them all for being such incredible role models and, indeed, SuperWomen!

As the saying goes 'everything is subject to change' and for us, these past few years have certainly proven that. You never know what lies ahead and as clichéd as it sounds it is important to remind ourselves to seize the moment and live each day. It is our dream that this book is every woman's reminder to do just that.

From Jodie

I consider myself very blessed to have so many wonderful people in my life to thank. There are lots of people who have been a great influence on my life to date and I am grateful to each person for all the positive (and not so positive!) experiences, as they have moulded me into who I am today.

A special acknowledgement to my wonderful 'husband-to-be' Peter. We are expecting our first baby as this inspirational book goes to print and I have never been happier. Pete is my greatest teacher and my best friend. We share so many goals, dreams and aspirations and I am looking forward to travelling through this life, hand in hand, to achieve each one of them. Thank you Pete. I love you.

I am very blessed to have such wonderful parents Denny and Mary who have loved me unconditionally, guided me continually and been my greatest friends. I am still my Daddy's little girl and my Mum is by far my greatest inspiration. If I can be half the parents they are, I will be very happy! My beautiful brother Craig who is so amazing, kind and giving. Without exception Craig is always there for me! I love you all so much.

I would like to thank those people who have made a significant impact on my career – Ron Jelich, Emmanuel and Julie Cassimatis from Storm Financial who are inspirational individuals, ethical, trustworthy and all mentors to me professionally.

A big thank you to Pete's family, my wonderful clients - you all know who you are - and fabulous friends for their consistent love, trust and support.

And finally, to my wonderful friends the LIPS girls - Rachael, Cyndi, Kim, Fleur and Allie - each of you are such amazing, talented and special women and I am truly grateful to have you in my life!

From Allison Mooney

I cannot begin to say how much I have appreciated the opportunity to be part of team who are passionate about life, not just for themselves but, for the well being of others in body, soul and spirit.

I am humbled by the extraordinary capacity that Rachael, Jodie, Cyndi, Kim and Fleur operate out of. Their generosity of spirit flows from their natural talents and abilities beyond their own backyard.

LIPS is not just another book, it has been born out of the lives of women who so want to leave a legacy. That is what motivates each one of us.

For me, I particularly want to dedicate this book to Brian, my husband and very best friend, who is my greatest champion —encouraging me when I'm exhausted or insecure and always finding humor to break tensions that come from the demands of life. My journey has been wonderful because you are part of it. We both know how the subject matter in this book adds to the success of our 39-year marriage.

My daughters Shay and Kyleigh are a gift from God to me. They are up there with breathing. I love you dearly, and I know you both have contributed to the way I see the world, and therefore you need to be acknowledged for your contribution to my efforts.

At the time of print I have one grandchild who gets me out of bed each day with such vigor. Josh you have an awesome spirit, and I wait with wonder as I see you emerge into a great leader and a brother to our newly awaited addition.

It starts and ends with family and as we move through life our families grow. LIPS girls you are a part of my family, you are remarkable, formidable women who are ready to set the world ablaze!

Author Profiles

Rachael Bermingham

Rachael Bermingham (nee Moore) lives on the Sunshine Coast with husband Paul (a renovator) & gorgeous son Jaxson 3. She is also 'wicked' step mum to Lee, 19 & Teri, 17.

Working from her home office, Rachael co-runs 4 Ingredients & Sunshine Coast Speakers & solo operates her personal speaking engagements & Read My Lips: her first self published book she co-wrote to inspire women to achieve their goals (first published 14/2/06) which she penned while feeding baby Jaxson.

A born entrepreneur Rachael showed her keen eye for business early opening her 1st business (the first mobile hair salon on the Sunshine Coast) at age 19.

After a 3 years of shark diving at Underwater World & 5 year stint as a Flight Centre travel agent, Rachael entered into what *could* have been considered a fatal business move by opening her own travel agency just 3 months *prior* to September 11. This experience would ultimately prove to be a pivotal point in her career, igniting the development of an ability which would be invaluable for Rachaels future professional career.

With the travel trade in a downward spiral, Rachael didn't give up; instead she worked long hours teaching herself how to market so her business would survive in the industry's most ruinous era. Researching & testing LOTS (& *LOTS!)* of strategies, she learnt the art of marketing &

found she LOVED it & *thankfully* had a real knack for it.

Her talent for marketing & publicity soon became well known and requests from others to help them also started coming in. Rachael left the travel industry to take on the first of many businesses she would build from a tiny turnover to an *astonishing* MULTI MILLION dollar turnover within months AND *without* spending a cent on advertising! During this time she was also a director various business boards,

Within days of becoming a Mum Rachael, known for her abundant energy & enthusiasm, continued to pursue her passion for business, instigating a motivational seminar for women encompassing life, health, wealth and business success strategies with her friend and business partner Cyndi O'Meara that ran for two years and morphed into the book Read My Lips.

It was by giving Read My Lips to friend Kim McCosker as a gift at Jaxson's first birthday party that would prove to be the beginning of yet another incredible journey for Rachael. Prompted by Rachael's passing comment of 'They say everyone has a good book in them' Kim entrusted her own fabulous idea for a book with Rachael (a cookbook using only a few ingredients) and the 2 friends pooled their talents together and wrote what became the best selling cookbook in Australia in 2007 and 2008.

These days when Rachael's not enjoying time with her family, cooking up a storm with Kim, or working on other books, she loves speaking at conferences to inspire others to achieve their own goals. She also enjoys talking on time management, life balance, how to develop a business from home *and of course* marketing and publicity.

Contact Rachael at these website links;
Read My Lips; www.ReadMyLips.com
4 Ingredients; www.4ingredients.com.au
Speaking Information & bookings; www.RachaelBermingham.com
Sunshine Coast Speakers; www.SunshineCoastSpeakers.com
or by email; info@RachaelBermingham.com
or by snail mail; PO Box 1171 Mooloolaba QLD 4557

Cyndi O'Meara

Cyndi O'Meara is not your typical nutritionist. She disagrees with low-fat, low-calorie diets and she thinks chocolate can be good for you and coffee is not so bad. She loves butter. She is the 'one out of ten nutritionists' who does *not* recommend a certain breakfast cereal, and she thinks cheating and eating yummy food are all part of a well-balanced diet.

Cyndi must be doing something right because she maintains a healthy weight and has never (in her whole life!) taken an antibiotic, pain-killer or any other form of medication. Her children are aged 14, 17 and 19 and they too have no need for medications.

Cyndi inspires and encourages people to create new, simple and achievable habits to get the life and health they want. To have wonderful health and wellbeing is merely a matter of changing habits, habits that very few people practise, but everyone can.

Her qualifications include a Bachelor of Science degree majoring in Nutrition from Deakin University in Victoria and the University of Colorado in Boulder, Colorado, and postgraduate studies in human anatomy from RMIT Victoria. In 2003 Cyndi was named Sunshine Coast Business Woman of the Year.

Since the success of her two books Changing Habits, Changing Lives, and Changing Habits Changing Lives Cookbook, and the companion

Changing Habits Changing Lives Audio, Cyndi has been in demand both nationally and internationally as a keynote speaker and now spends time travelling and advocating her approach to holistic health and well-being.

Contact Cyndi at these website links:
Read My Lips; www.ReadMyLips.com
Changing Habits Changing Lives; www.ChangingHabits.com.au
Sunshine Coast Speakers; www.SunshineCoastSpeakers.com
or by email; cyndi@ChangingHabits.com.au
or by snail mail; PO Box 104 Mooloolaba Qld 4557 Australia.

Fleur Welligan & Kim Morrison

Taking care of yourself isn't selfish – it's essential! But when life gets busy and there is information overload, how on earth can we be expected to keep a healthy balance? Kim Morrison and Fleur Whelligan together bring over 28 years of experience in the health and wellbeing industry.

Authors, therapists, presenters and speakers, their message is about commitment and the hundreds of small but important choices you make every single day that impact on your attitude, your health and your wellbeing. Their three internationally acclaimed books: Like Chocolate for Women – Indulge and Recharge in Everyday Aromatherapy, Like An Apple A Day – Taking Care of Yourself for Health and Vitality and About Face – Look and Feel 10years Younger Naturally, have gained them credibility as world renowned health and lifestyle educators. The most popular topics they are asked to deliver are: Taking Care of Health before Taking Care of Business, How to Achieve the Magic Work/Life Balance, and Self Care in the 21st Century. Along with speaking they are sought after as MCs, and 'brain breathers'; offering dynamic session breaks that add the 'x' factor to any conference.

"Our vision is to educate and empower people to make positive practical choices regarding their health and well being; to inspire people to acknowledge that health and inner beauty is their greatest asset and to respect and live in harmony with all mother nature provides".

Contact Fleur and Kim at these website links;
Read My Lips; www.ReadMyLips.com
Creative Wellbeing; www.creativewellbeing.com
Speaking bookings; www.SunshineCoastSpeakers.com
or by email;   fleur@creativewellbeing.com
              kim@creativewellbeing.com
or by snail mail; PO Box 1192 Mooloolaba, Qld, Australia 4557.

Jodie McIver

Jodie McIver has been recognised as one of Australia's leading financial planners and is currently National Manager for Education Services for Australia's largest independent Financial Planning firm

Her love of helping people achieve financial freedom started over 10 years ago when, while working for a paralegal/conveyancer, she made the decision to move into financial planning. It has been her passion ever since, supported by her string of qualifications and impressive resume.

Jodie accumulated extensive experience in the financial planning industry with major firms and institutional banks in Brisbane and on the Sunshine Coast, Queensland. Her personal, yet professional manner generated a very loyal client base and she was recognised nationally within these adviser roles. Having achieved great success in one of the major banks in Australia, Jodie joined the team at one of Australia's leading financial firms, Storm Financial in early 2005. She established the Sunshine Coast office in 2006 and continues to achieve outstanding results, thriving on Storm's philosophy to proactively generate wealth for all clients.

To support her experience, Jodie's continues her education to keep abreast of current legislation and trends and is currently undertaking a Master's of Business Applied Finance with QUT. She believes education is an essential component to people's ability to achieve results.

Alongside her passion for finance is Jodie's love for horses and she strives to start a few days of the week with an early morning ride on her horse which she believes helps balance her mind and soul. She also enjoys spending time with both family and friends entertaining in a magnificent ocean view home she recently built with her partner Peter.

Together they both make the most of the fantastic lifestyle the Sunshine Coast has to offer.

Contact Jodie at these website links;
Read My Lips; www.ReadMyLips.com
Storm Financial; www.StormFinancial.com.au
or by email; jodie.mciver@StormFinancial.com.au
or by snail mail; PO Box 650 Maroochydore QLD 4558

Allison Mooney

Allison Mooney is the Author of "Pressing The Right Buttons" which has become an International best seller. She is also an International Corporate Speaker, her favourite topic being "people skills for business success'. Allison understands people like "Fisherman know their fish!"

She holds impressive speaking awards such as; 'Speaker of the year' twice (a first in the history of NSANZ) 2004-2005, 'Most Entertaining & Humorous Speaker' 2006, and Most Inspirational Speaker of the Year 2007.

She is a passionate and endearing writer who infuses a desire in her readers to significantly increase their own performance capability, while constantly improving the quality of their lives, and the lives of those with whom they come in contact with. Allison speaks in both New Zealand and Australia helping people to gain a greater understanding and respect of each other, their strengths and motivations.

Her topics include;

- 'Speed reading' others to find out what they really want.
- Talking to others in a way that makes them want to listen.
- How to relate more by seeing things through others eyes.

Contact Allison at these website links;
Read My Lips; www.ReadMyLips.com
Website; www.personalityplus.co.nz
Speaking bookings; www.sunshinecoastspeakers.com
or by email; info@personalityplus.co.nz
or by snail mail; 13 Glamorgan Drive Torbay Auckland New Zealand

Bibliography

4 Ingredients: Rachael Bermingham and Kim McCosker, self-published March 2007

4 Ingredients 2: Rachael Bermingham and Kim McCosker, self-published August 2008

Changing Habits Changing Lives: Cyndi O'Meara, Penguin 1998

Changing Habits Changing Lives Cookbook: Cyndi O'Meara, Penguin 2002

Like Chocolate For Women: Kim Morrison & Fleur Whelligan, Tandem Press, 2001

Like An Apple A Day: Kim Morrison & Fleur Whelligan, Tandem Press, 2003

About Face: Kim Morrison & Fleur Whelligan, Random House, 2006

Pushing The Right Buttons: Allison Mooney, Random House, 2008

The Secret: Rhonda Byrne, Simon and Schuster 2007

Excuse Me Your Life is Waiting For You: June Grabhorn, Hodder 2004

Ask and It is Given: Esther Hicks, Hay House 2004

Personality Plus: Florence Littauer, Monarch Books, 1983

Notes

Notes